Hey...

I

Believe

In

YOU!

THE
ANSWER
DISCOVERY

How to Change the World
by Helping Others
...and Ourselves

PAUL WHITE

Published by The Answer Discovery, Inc.
www.theanswerdiscovery.com

The Answer Discovery, Inc. is committed to preserving and protecting the natural resources of the earth. Environmentally responsible and sustainable practices are pursued and embraced in all the company does.

Library of Congress Cataloging-in-Publication

ISBN 979-8-9882375-0-1 (Paperback)

Visit the author's website: www.theanswerdiscovery.com

DISCLAIMER

This publication is designed to provide general information regarding the subject matter covered. Neither the author nor the publisher assume any responsibility for any errors or omissions, nor do they represent or warrant that the information, ideas, plans, actions, suggestions, and methods of operation contained herein are in all cases true, accurate, appropriate, or legal. It is the reader's responsibility to consult with his or her own advisor before putting any of the enclosed information, ideas, or practices into play. The author and the publisher specifically disclaim any liability resulting from the use or application of the information contained in this book, and the information is not intended to serve as legal advice related to a person's individual situation.

This book is based on the author's life experiences, opinion, and knowledge gained from the constant pursuit of excellence. Names, characters, places, and incidents are either the product of the author's imagination or are used fictitiously. Any resemblance to actual persons, living or dead, or to actual events or locales is entirely coincidental.

CONTENTS

. . .

Preface: The Power of One 7

Introduction 13

1. The Gift of Perspective Management 17

2. The Gift of Living Life Helping Others 39

3. The Gift of Relationships 51

4. The Gift of Telling the Truth and Owning a Mistake 73

5. The Gift and Power of Forgiveness 97

6. The Gift of Being Chosen for the Privilege 119

7. The Gift of Modeling 153

8. The Gift of Mentoring 169

9. The Gift of Gratitude 187

Acknowledgments 201

About the Author 203

THE POWER OF ONE

D o you believe in the "power of one"? *I do!* So much so that I wrote this book to prove its existence and value. Are you the "one with the power"? *I believe you are!* Everything you do and say matters. Everything you post on the internet matters. Not just to you, but to all of us. And to all future generations. Want proof? Of course you do, because you've received valuable training in how to be skeptical.

Okay, here's proof: Pause for a moment, think of an individual who had a positive impact on your life in some way, and call them now. Yes, right now. Tell them two things: how they made a positive difference in your life, and how grateful you are that they did. Don't keep reading. Stop right now; do it. Make the call.

When you've completed this simple task, ask yourself this question: Did the life of the person you just called *improve or get worse* because of the call? It's impossible that it stayed the same. If you followed the instructions and you were sincere, the only possible result is that it *improved*. Now *that's* power! And *you* possess it.

Still skeptical? Okay, go perform a random act of kindness and analyze the results of that random act. Funny, isn't it? When I asked you to analyze the results, I'm guessing that the results you analyzed only involved the recipient of the random act of kindness and didn't include yourself. But science indicates it's impossible to perform a random act of kindness and not experience our own release of serotonin—that internal product we all possess that gives us a feeling of euphoric joy. There's your proof. That's the "power of one"!

Life has taught me thousands of valuable lessons. I want to share the most impactful lessons with you. This book contains nine "gifts" that you can give to yourself and then, through your own life, to others. Take note that each of the nine gifts contains its own collection of valuable life lessons. If you read this entire book and only take one life lesson away, it may be the lesson that changes the world, through you, forever. Here's how I know that can happen. Consider the following story:

> A woman was attending a three-day seminar at an ocean-side resort. After the first day was complete, she went up to her room, located on the twelfth floor, to relax for an hour before she met other attendees for dinner. She approached the balcony that looked out onto the ocean and took in the incredible view of the water. As her gaze lowered to the beautiful sugar-white sand beach, she noticed what appeared to be a dark stripe about six feet wide running up and down the beach for as far as she could see in both directions. She couldn't make out what the stripe was, and intrigue got the better of her. She went down to the lobby and exited the resort to further investigate.

> The six-foot line was only about three feet from the edge of the water, and as she moved closer to the shore, she realized that the line was made up of starfish. There were hundreds of them right in front of her, and as she glanced up and down the shore, she couldn't see an end to the

line! About a hundred yards to her right, she saw what appeared to be a young man or boy who kept bending over the stripe made up of starfish, then standing up and swinging his arms. She wondered what he was doing, so she headed in his direction.

When she was about twenty yards away, she realized that he was picking up individual starfish and throwing them out into the water. She continued to approach him. She figured that the boy in front of her was maybe twelve, thirteen at the most. Now just a few feet away, she said, "Hi there. What are you doing?" The boy looked up at her, smiled, and continued picking up starfish and throwing them into the ocean as he replied, "You may have heard that yesterday there were some massive solar flares on the sun's surface."

He didn't wait for her to respond as he continued, "Well, those massive solar flares have an impact on the earth's magnetic field. The earth's magnetic field is what controls the timing of the ocean's tide inflow and outflow. Members of the aquatic world have routines, just like us humans, only for some of them, like starfish, their routines are based on the timing consistencies of the tide flow. When the tide comes in, the starfish follow it onto the beach to feed. They move slowly but know exactly when they need to move away from the beach so that they don't get trapped. When a massive solar flare affects the earth's magnetic pull, it alters the timing of the tide for a couple of days. All of these starfish got caught because of their dependence on the tide consistency. If they're out of the water too long, they'll die, so I'm throwing them back into the water to save their lives."

The woman couldn't believe what she had just been told, but it all made sense. She looked up and down the beach, then back at the young boy, and said, "But there must be thousands and thousands of starfish stuck on the beach. What you're doing can't possibly make a difference." Just then the boy reached down, picked up another starfish, threw it in the ocean, paused, then looked at her and said, "It made a difference to *that* one." He reached down, grabbing another, and continued his mission. The woman realized that he was focused on the starfish he *was* saving rather than the ones he wasn't. Then she suddenly realized that *one* counts—that is, even if you can only help one, it matters.

The starfish story ends with the woman realizing that her mind had been focused on the logic of what she was experiencing rather than pursuing the wisdom of what the moment offered. It would end up being her greatest takeaway from the seminar. She paused, locked the lesson of the moment in her memory bank, embraced the joy of the moment, and ended up kindly asking the young boy, "Can I help?"

It was the starfish story that convinced me that we all have power. It showed that it doesn't matter whether we win or lose; what matters most is that we make the attempt, that we at least try, that we give our very best effort. It's never failure until someone gives up. Winners never fail; they either win or they learn.

You can learn a lot from reading this book. Life lessons can come from anywhere. I learned another of my most powerful lessons while watching the Pixar movie *Toy Story 2* with my kids when they were young. The animated movie begins with a dinosaur toy named Rex playing a video game, utilizing his friend Buzz Lightyear's toy character to battle Buzz's arch-nemesis toy, the evil emperor Zurg. Rex ends up getting Buzz killed, which results in losing the game. In frustration, Rex complains to Buzz about how he always loses. Later in the movie, Rex finds a secret code book showing how Buzz can defeat Zurg in the game. Then he discovers Buzz right in the middle of a real-life fight with Zurg and screams the solution: *"You just have to believe in yourself!"*

And that's the lesson, gifted to me by a movie intended to entertain kids. Funny, isn't it? As humans we are so very capable of accomplishing a life far beyond our wildest dreams, if only we can believe in ourselves or be supported and inspired by others who believe in us. The book you're holding can take you from where you are to where you always dreamed you could be, if you'll simply open and unpack the gifts it contains and take the action that puts them into immediate use in your life. Don't worry if you're struggling with believing in yourself as you begin this journey. I believe in the "power of one," and *I believe in you!*

Paul

INTRODUCTION

The tears had begun to run down his cheeks again. He had recently realized that his favorite and most powerful emotion was "joy that moved him to tears." It was kind of a sub-emotion of gratitude. The combination of joy and gratitude, working together, had motivated and inspired everything he had accomplished in his adult life. He knew today was the day: his final day on earth. He was aware of the signals his broken body had been sending to his brain. His wonderful brain—such a fragile instrument that each of us possess. It works both day and night, managing our physical and mental health. How can one ever properly pay homage to the most powerful part of our being—the part of us that we seemingly least understand?

Well ... a few months ago, before illness had anchored him to his bed, he'd figured it out. Now he was about to share what would be his final idea for helping all of mankind, and he was attempting to control his overwhelming feeling of joy as he was given the opportunity, with complete clarity, to pass this idea on to his son Peter, who he knew would share it with the world. He was so grateful that they had repaired the relationship that at one point in time had almost ceased to exist. As he was about to enter the afterlife, he knew their relationship had never been better. He smiled and let the tears flow. His idea was simple: There would be a place, accessible to all, that would direct people to the answers they sought for the things they could not solve on their own. It would be called the Answer Discovery.

Just then, Peter walked into the room of his home where his father, who he so loved, would finish his earthly journey. "Wonderful morning, Awesome Father," escaped softly from Peter's lips as he noticed the streaks of tears flowing down his dad's cheeks into the pillow that his head lay upon. "Your smile reveals the truth. I see you're beginning yet another day with tears of joy this morning. How 'bout sharing your thoughts that are leading to this incredible joy?"

"Today is my day, Son! I've prepared myself to finish my earthly journey with a full and loving heart and a mind that has found total peace. I have one thing left to do today before I pass on."

Peter sat on the side of his father's bed and gently took his father's hand. Reveling in the incredible gift of being the son of the man before him, he looked deep into his father's eyes. It had been so hard to put into words the connection they had with each other.

It hadn't always been that way. Their relationship had endured years of pain as they navigated the inevitable challenges that children experience with their parents. But neither of them ever totally gave up on each other, and, with the help of time, they were able to find a sweet spot that allowed the relationship to flourish. Now, savoring the power of the moment, Peter spoke to his father in a way they had developed with each other, always showing the love, appreciation, and respect they had for each other. Then Peter asked, "So, oh Wise One, just what is this momentous thing that you must do today for the privilege of finishing your journey in your normal kind and loving way?"

"I've found the answers, Son! The answers to all of the questions we as humans struggle to find ourselves."

"You mean like medical cures and everything?"

"No, the answers to all of the questions that prevent us humans from living a daily life filled with consistent joy, love, gratitude, peace, and hope. You see, every answer lies within a person who has *already experienced a life challenge that they successfully conquered* and who is willing to help those who have yet to find the answer to the same challenge. There is never a need to reinvent the wheel, *only a quest to correctly match people together.* There's a letter I've left you on my computer. Contained within that letter, you'll find the plans for a building, its purpose, how it will function, and, most importantly, the *why* behind it all. I'm leaving you the resources to build the first one as a gift to our community, which has meant so much to our family. Once it is established, and people realize the positive change it has on the lives of its community members, communities from all over the world will seek you out to help them build one in their community. And help them you will. Son, your greatest joy in life is yet to come. Embrace every moment of it."

Now tears of joy were running down Peter's face as he again looked deep into his father's eyes and said, "I love you, Dad!" His father closed his eyes, smiled gently, and softly replied, "I love you, Son." Right at that moment, the older man's earthly odyssey reached its conclusion, as Peter laid his head on his father's chest, gave him one last embrace, and quietly whispered, "See you at the top, Dad!"

THE GIFT OF PERSPECTIVE MANAGEMENT

heila was driving her third circle around the block, and the lone parking space was still open. She had driven by the space three times yesterday but just couldn't will herself to pull in. She had almost hoped that her Mercedes would take control of itself and pull in for her, but alas, it was not to be. Finally, Sheila decided that just pulling in didn't really commit her to anything. After all, it was just a regular city parking space, just like the hundreds of others around the city she had grown up in. But she also knew that this one was special. This was the lone parking place for the structure called the Answer Discovery.

Sheila had read about it. She had heard about it. But frankly she was a little uncertain about it, and she sat there wondering if she wanted to enter out of sheer curiosity or if she was finally willing to admit she needed help. Here she was, just thirty-seven years old, hearing from all of these other people that she "had it *all*." The "all" they were referring to included a successful career by "career standards," significant wealth by "wealth standards," loving husband by "loving husband standards," and three overachieving children based, she guessed, on "overachieving children standards." All she knew was that the way she felt right now, right at this precise moment, you could heap all of those things on one side of a scale, and it would show that the emptiness she felt inside weighed twice as much. She knew that the desperation of trying to find herself with an "is this all there is?" attitude had begun to overwhelm her thoughts every minute of every day. She was consumed by these thoughts, and out of despair she pulled into the parking place that seemed to beckon to her.

Once Sheila parked, she couldn't bring herself to get out and approach the building. She began to cry and whispered, "Why me, why me, why me?" Several times each day she went through a pattern of frustration knowing she "had it all," and the only thing that *having it all* had resulted in was a feeling of emptiness. Just as she reached for a tissue to dry her tears, she witnessed an elderly man trip and fall on the sidewalk right next to her car. She jumped out of her car, without noticing whether there were any cars coming, and rushed to his aid. He had managed to catch his forward fall with his hands outstretched but had scraped the palms of his hands pretty severely, and they began to bleed. As Sheila began to attend to him and his injured hands, she remembered she had some unopened bottles of water in her car that she could utilize to help clean the wounds and that her fancy car came with a first aid kit. She had never used the first aid kit before, but suddenly she was grateful that it was there.

The elderly gentleman was a little embarrassed that he had fallen but extremely grateful that Sheila was helping him. "I don't know how I can be so clumsy and lucky at the same time," he said.

Sheila responded, "What do you mean?"

"As I've gotten older, I have a diminished ability to do the things I used to do subconsciously. Now I have to concentrate just to walk successfully. That's the clumsy part. But lo and behold, an angel was nearby to help me through the physical and mental pain that resulted from my clumsiness. I only wish I wasn't providing the big guy above with so many opportunities to dispense his army of angels. Are you an angel often?"

Sheila looked deep into the elderly gentleman's eyes as the emotions that had been interrupted by his fall returned, and she burst into tears.

"Whoa now, hey there, it's okay," he said. "It isn't often that angels cry. Would it help if I fell again?"

"No, no, I'm so sorry, I ... I'm ... I've just had a lot on my mind, and I stopped because I was going to ... Well, I had heard that this building ... or that this place here was somehow helping people in strange ways ... and I think, well I guess, I need help figuring life ... I mean *my* life ... well, actually, life in general ... out."

"Fascinating," the elderly gentleman replied. "An angel in need of an angel. Well, young woman, I am indebted to your random act of kindness for taking care of my hands and hope that I have an opportunity to pay your kindness forward. In the meantime, having interrupted your journey from your vehicle to the New Life Palace, it would do my heart good if you would get back to your original intention and seek an answer to questions you seem to have burning inside of you."

"You just called it the New Life Palace. I thought it was called the Answer Discovery," said Sheila.

The kindly old gentleman replied, "Oh, it *is* called the Answer Discovery and that's its proper name, but I live around the corner and have witnessed enough happenings from the day it opened that I affectionately call it the New Life Palace. May I watch you enter? You're so close to the answers you seek that I would hate to see you turn around now."

Sheila replied, "Well, yes ... I ... I mean sure. Okay, sure." She looked deep into the elderly gentleman's warm eyes and knew that he would wait there until she entered. She paused, slowly took in a breath of air, turned toward the entrance to the Answer Discovery, and approached the door. As she grabbed the door handle, she glanced over at the loving, compassionate face of the man she had just helped. His face was wearing a smile that seemed to be encouraging her to enter. And so she pulled open the door and entered the Answer Discovery.

The first thing Sheila noticed was the floor. It almost seemed transparent, and when she gazed right in front of her she saw a word shining—no, not shining, *glowing*—from the floor. The word was HOPE, and it appeared as though it had a pulsating glow that mirrored the rate of her heartbeat. Sheila took all of this in for about twenty seconds, and then the word WELCOME appeared in front of her eyes. She immediately felt strange. Not strange in a bad way, like she needed to run. It was almost a calmness—a feeling that she hadn't felt since she was a girl. Still, she jumped when all of a sudden she sensed that she heard the words How MIGHT I SERVE YOU? come out of thin air. She quickly realized that she hadn't actually *heard* them but that they kind of appeared to her in a soft and comforting kind of way.

Before she even knew what she wanted to say, Sheila blurted out, "I want to be happy and I don't know how. Please, please help me. I just don't know what to do anymore." She sensed the words PLEASE CONTINUE. And she did. "I know I should be happy. I know I've experienced every form of success. But none of it matters anymore. I constantly feel overwhelmed and underappreciated. I don't feel loved, even though I know people love me. I just don't respect myself. It all seems like a lie. Please, please…I need help. Is there anything you can do for me? I mean, I don't even know who you are or how this works. I'm not even sure why I'm here. Maybe I shouldn't have come. I'm so sorry. I didn't want to trouble you. I…I…"

The tears began to flow. Sheila was beginning to feel spent. Now she felt bad that she had even entered. She decided to blurt out one last plea: "Please, please, can you help me?" And then … nothing. Silence began to build, first in the room and then inside of her. She was beginning to feel ashamed that she felt the way she did, knowing that she had been given so much in life. She began to turn around and move toward the door, but the door that had been there when she entered … wasn't there anymore. As she slowly turned herself in a circle, she couldn't see any exit but realized that she didn't really want to leave this place. What a quandary of emotions.

Suddenly, words came to her. THANK YOU FOR CHOOSING TO ENTER THE ANSWER DISCOVERY TODAY. THANK YOU ALSO FOR HELPING WALLY RIGHT BEFORE COMING IN. IT REVEALED SO MUCH ABOUT WHO YOU REALLY ARE. I REQUEST THAT YOU VISIT JANE MARTIN. SHE'LL BE WORKING TOMORROW FROM TEN IN THE MORNING UNTIL ABOUT TWO IN THE AFTERNOON AND WILL APPRECIATE YOUR ASSISTANCE. YOU'LL WANT TO BE PROMPT, AND THE ADDRESS YOU'LL BE LOOKING FOR IS 412 W. BUTTLES STREET. JANE WILL BE EXPECTING YOU."

All of a sudden, Sheila felt different. She had been given an assignment. She knew she was good at pursuing and completing assignments. She glanced to her left and saw the exit. As she took her first step toward the door, she seemed to have the words APPRECIATION, RESPECT, and LOVE flash in front of her from the surface of the floor. Then she exited the Answer Discovery.

"Yup! You've got it. It's the beginning of the look," said Wally. He had gone home, gotten a lightweight folding chair and a glass of iced tea, and had perched himself right outside the door to the New Life Palace, as he liked to refer to it. "You supposed to go someplace?" he inquired.

"Yes," Sheila answered. "Tomorrow, although I'm not quite sure why, and I don't really know what's in store for me, but I want to go and for some strange reason I feel like there may be hope … and answers to the questions that persist in my mind."

"Then you must go and follow what your heart is telling you to do. Peace to you, my sister...and thanks for being my angel earlier. As you can see, my hands are gonna heal just fine." And with that Wally stood up, grabbed his chair and glass of iced tea, and headed toward his home.

Sheila paused for a minute and watched him walk away. Funny, she thought, she couldn't remember pausing for a minute at any time in the last several years. She smiled, gently walked toward her car, and began the journey home, excited for what lay ahead of her tomorrow.

• • •

As Sheila looked for numbers on the houses on both sides of the street, she realized that the number she was looking for would be on her left, as it was an even number. This was an older part of town, and had its share of homes that were in need of some tender loving care, but it was still regarded as a safe part of town. She had begun the morning filled with curiosity and excitement. As she approached the 400 block, she began to realize that she was very close to where she believed a homeless shelter was. Another two hundred yards, and her excitement turned into a little bit of apprehension when she saw the numbers 412 on a building that was, indeed, a homeless shelter. She hesitated as she wondered if this was actually where she was supposed to be, but a little unwanted help from a vehicle that came up close behind and put its horn to the test prompted her to turn into a drive that led to a tight parking area that was wide enough for only about four vehicles.

Sheila double-checked the numbers and realized that this *was* the address she was supposed to arrive at that day. She hoped finding this woman named Jane would be easy. Realizing how far this was taking her out of her normal comfort zone, she wondered to herself how she could feel so confident in some situations and so insecure in others. She was about to open her door and exit her vehicle when, all of a sudden, someone was standing right next to it, trying to say something to her. It frightened her at first as she looked out her vehicle's window into the face of a man who hadn't shaved in a couple of weeks. He was wearing clothes that sorely needed some cleaning and maybe a little mending too. As she tried to understand what he was saying, she lowered her car window about an inch to prevent him from being able to reach in.

"I was trying to ask if you were here to help cook today," said the man. "Because if you are, I wanted to see if I could make a special request for lunch."

"Hey, Tom," came a woman's voice from a side entrance door. "You'll be happy to know that we'll be making some of our homemade mac and cheese today. I know it's your favorite."

"YES!" said the man emphatically.

"Well, don't just stand there. Open the door for the lady so she can get in here and get started," said the woman. Sheila heard this and began to get out of her car. Tom grabbed the door and helped swing it open while gently saying, "Right this way, milady. Anyone who's here to help with my all-time favorite dish deserves the royal treatment."

"Oh, I don't think I'm who you're thinking I am. I'm just here to meet with a Jane Martin," said Sheila.

"And meet with her you're about to," Tom responded. "She's that lovely lady right over there." Jane was walking over from the side door with an outstretched hand that had the palm half-turned toward the sky. It was a warm handshake that immediately lowered Sheila's anxiety.

"Welcome. You must be Sheila. I'm Jane. What a privilege to meet with you today and to have you here to help. Thanks ever so much for showing up a few minutes early. We've got plenty to do to keep our schedule," said Jane.

Sheila responded, "I'm not quite sure I understand. I know I'm supposed to meet with you today, but I don't know how I can be of help. I…I … Well, the truth is, I was kinda coming here for help from you. At least I *thought* I was."

"The best way I know how to accomplish the task I've been given for meeting with you is for me to enlist your help in the other task I'm in charge of today. That task is preparing a midday meal for all the people that are about to show up in just about two hours," said Jane. "I need you to wash your hands real good, put on some of those food service gloves, and since you didn't come in wearing a baseball cap I'm gonna need you to start a new fashion trend and place one of those lovely hair nets over there on top of that beautiful head of hair you brought with you today."

Everything was happening so fast that Sheila didn't have time to recognize just how far out of her comfort zone she was. Entranced with this woman named Jane, she simply complied with all that she was being told to do. Although her mind was temporarily distracted, she was starting to feel like the answers she was seeking were about to be revealed.

"One of the primaries today is going to be chicken stoup! I know it's a funny name, but it accurately describes the goal of what I want it to be. It's not soup and it's not stew; it's *stoup*! And you won't find any better in the land than the stoup you're about to prepare." Jane was on a roll. "In that five-gallon pot over there on the stove we're boiling about three dozen chicken breasts that will be ready for chopping in about ten more minutes. I've got just the right amount of water in there and the perfect amount of Frankenmuth Chicken seasoning that I brought from home. You and I are going to take the next twenty minutes and start dicing carrots, celery, zucchini, Vidalia onion, and a little bit of asparagus. Open that large storage container over there in the corner and see what our inventory of noodles looks like."

Sheila began to move toward the corner and asked, "How many people will we be feeding?"

Jane smiled. It hadn't gone unnoticed that Sheila had just utilized the word *we* rather than *you* in the question she had just asked. It was a good sign. She knew she already had "buy-in" and that Sheila was opening up and preparing for the discussion that was about to ensue. "Most likely somewhere between fifty and seventy, including the kids. What do we have for noodles that we can use?"

"I counted thirty packages of wide egg noodles, forty-two boxes of spaghetti noodles, and five boxes of angel hair pasta," said Sheila after a couple of minutes of counting. "What would you like to utilize?"

Jane replied, "I just love those wide egg noodles. Let's start with five bags of those and see what it looks like. We'll add them in about twenty minutes prior to the time we start serving. We'll have a good boil going by then, and they should be perfect for our stoup. You can set the bags right on the counter over there, so they're ready to go when we need them, and then why don't you go ahead and help me get started with the chopping here? I just finished sharpening up some of the knives and have the other primary dish, which today will be seven pans of homemade mac and cheese with our secret ingredients, bacon and triple cheese, in the oven and baking. I'd like to begin talking with you about the things that brought you here today. We can change your entire life and world right here while we prepare the not-yet-world-famous chicken stoup this morning."

Sheila was caught off guard by the statement Jane had just made. How could it be that this woman she had just met could solve all the pain she had been suffering for such a long period of time? They began the chopping.

"So according to my preparation it seems that you've got the perfect life—according to everyone except for the person that matters most, which would be *you*," began Jane. "And if I understand it correctly, you're not real happy about all of the great things happening in your life, even though our society says you should be. Am I close?"

Sheila immediately wished she was dicing onions rather than the carrots she was working on so she had a semi-legitimate excuse for the tears that started to flow. "You're spot on," she said. It was a phrase that she used often at work and home. Jane kept the discussion moving. "That's absolutely wonderful, because you are precisely at a place that I was five years ago. Or, if you prefer, five years ago I was the person you are today, and I know exactly what's wrong and what you can do about it to turn it around forever. You suffer from *perspective flaw,* and I've got just the cure."

"What do you mean, I have perspective flaw?" responded Sheila.

"What I mean is that you have a subconscious misutilization of the 'perspective genetics gift' that was provided to you but never properly trained. It's kind of like a dog. If a dog isn't trained *where* to go when it *needs* to go, where does it usually go? In the wrong place, right?" said Jane.

"I … I guess so," answered Sheila, slightly confused as she attempted to listen and chop carrots for the stoup at the same time.

Jane continued:

"Achieving desired outcomes must include the proper training in the use of the tools provided. Have you ever tried to pound in a nail with the handle end of the hammer? Of course not, because you were trained at some point in your life to know that the metal end was most effective. Not only the metal end but the flat circular part of the metal end, and not the claw part, which you learned is used to *remove* nails.

"Here's another example. When you tie your shoes, do you still go through each and every step the way you were trained? You remember, don't you? Put one shoelace in each hand, overlap the two laces, feed one lace through the hole that was created between the overlap and the shoe, grab the end of each lace and pull until tight, then form a loop … and on and on until you complete the tying of the shoe. Then repeat for the other shoe.

"Isn't it absolutely amazing that, once we are trained, we can allow our subconscious mind to complete this task over and over again while allowing our conscious mind to focus on something totally different? That's plenty of carrots. Let's get to work on chopping some of the zucchini."

After they shifted the chopped carrots over on the cutting board and began working on the zucchini, Jane resumed her speech. "So if we can take the mental tools that we were provided with and train them so that we both utilize them correctly for the purpose they were intended for and practice the correct utilization repeatedly until our subconscious becomes able to take control and become the default response, then we can consistently achieve the desired outcome."

Jane paused the conversation with Sheila for a second. "Hey, George," Jane said to another volunteer who had just arrived. "Welcome. Thanks for being here again this week. You are one awesome dude. Can you please turn the ovens on to 350 degrees to preheat them? We're having my not-yet-famous mac-and-cheese-cheese-cheese fully supported by bacon today."

"Welcome yourself, Superwoman. Don't we usually cook mac and cheese at 325, and what the heck is mac-and-cheese-cheese-cheese fully supported by bacon?" George responded.

"Regarding cooking the mac and cheese, yes, but we didn't get it out of the freezer as early as we should have, and it will only be ready on time if we turn up the heat a little. Plus, it's my 'm-triple-c plus bacon,' which, I'll have you know, some people consider taste bud heaven. How's your 'giddy up' today?" inquired Jane.

"It's just like I'm wearing a custom-made suit in an off-the-rack world," George shot back. Jane smiled and turned her attention back to Sheila and the chopping they were both performing.

"Correct and classic utilization of the perspective gene derived from dedicated training and consistent practice, which subsequently transformed into the most beneficial subconscious response. I love that guy!" Jane said, smiling widely.

"Excuse me?" It was more of a "what the heck did you just say" statement than a question from Sheila.

"In much simpler terms," Jane quipped, "He *gets* it! Like I said, I came here about five years ago in a situation similar to yours. Many things going right in my life but just not happy. George trained me on the secret to instant perspective change. I locked the secret into my brain, began practicing it immediately, and transformed myself into consistently living a wonderful life filled with joy each day, regardless of the circumstances that I'm engaged in. Now I devote some time each day attempting to pay the secret forward to others just like you."

Sheila had been chopping away at a faster and faster pace as Jane had been talking. She abruptly stopped, looked up at Jane with the saddest of eyes, and asked, "Jane . . . will you share the secret with me?"

"That's precisely why you're here," stated Jane. "But we have a large group of hungry people showing up in about an hour, and we need to be prepared to serve them. If you can stay focused on the moment over the next two hours, the secret that I'll continue to share with you when we're done serving food will make more sense. Let's see if that chicken is ready to be chopped, and let's 'giddy up' with the world's best stoup that's ever been created."

Sheila, George, and Jane were part of a group of six volunteers that worked hard and efficiently at preparing a meal for the fifty to seventy expected diners that day. The two "primaries," consisting of "mac-and-cheese-cheese-cheese fully supported with bacon" along with the awesomely developed "chicken stoup" were ready to go at

11:55 a.m., as was a large bowl of fruit salad, a large bowl of taco salad that a local Mexican restaurant had donated and dropped off in the morning, and three large pans of apple crisp that had already solicited nine "Wow, does that ever smell good" comments from the volunteers. Jane smiled as she thought about how three of them had said it twice. At three minutes prior to the noon hour, George gathered together the volunteers and began praying, as was tradition before each meal at the shelter, saying, "Heavenly Father, we are grateful…" which Jane followed with "… that Sheila could be with us today and for her open heart and mind."

"For my wife's tolerance to the chemotherapy treatment she received this week and that my health is so good," said another volunteer. Shelia looked around and noticed that everyone else's head was bowed and their eyes were closed.

"That I received help from my teacher, which led to a B-plus on my history exam this week," said a young boy whom Sheila thought she had recognized earlier as a classmate of one her daughters from the local high school.

"And Lord, I'm grateful that I have a job when so many are unemployed," quipped another.

"I'm grateful that I have a car when I know so many in this world have to walk miles just to get a day's ration of clean water. Thank you, Father."

"And I'm grateful that my opportunity clock went off again this morning in time for me to be here to help serve again today," said a man who looked to be over eighty but moved with the skill of a thirty-five-year-old.

After everyone except Sheila had expressed something they were grateful for, George finished with, "Father, for these things and for the gift of perspective we humbly offer our service to others with gratitude to you." And everyone present said together, "Amen."

As they prepared to start serving the people that were already twenty deep in line, waiting for the noon-hour meal, Sheila looked at Jane and said, "What's an opportunity clock?" Jane laughed, then chuckled because she had asked George that very same question the first time *she* had heard someone use the term *opportunity clock.*

"Well, I'm told it's a term that an awesome man with a funny name used to utilize to show people that there existed a totally different perspective from the one they had permanently cemented in their mind. Let's let this initial line of hungry folk get through and then I'll explain it a little deeper. It kind of represents the main reason you're here today," Jane said.

The first twenty-five or so people who had been present when the clock struck twelve had moved through the food line and were eating. Others began to slowly trickle in, and it gave Jane an opportunity to converse with Sheila while they served the food they had prepared.

"I had the same perspective flaw that you are currently battling. I didn't even realize that there's a war going on inside of our brain every day. It's a perspective war, and George shared with me that the first person he had heard mention this war was a man named Zig Ziglar, who believed that we had the ability to instantly change our perspective on *anything* that we perceive as negative. It all begins with our self-talk, and it's totally controlled by the words we choose when we talk to ourselves throughout every minute of each day."

Sheila interrupted at this point and said, "I'm not sure I'm following you, Jane. You said a couple of hours ago that I had a perspective flaw. What does that have to do with self-talk?"

"Great question," replied Jane.

"It leads right into a key point: The conversations we have with ourselves each day are more important than the conversations we have with others. This is due to the direct impact our self-talk has on the success of everything we say, do, write, or post on the internet each day. Most every person I know calls it an alarm clock. The word *alarm* is associated with terms including *sudden fright, apprehension, notice of danger, bell, buzzer, call to arms, frighten,* and *warn of danger.*

"Zig changed the thing that wakes us up in the morning to an opportunity clock. The word *opportunity* is associated with terms such as *favorable time or condition* and *good chance.* Don't you see? Just changing one word takes a negative perspective and turns it into a positive perspective. What a difference it makes when your opportunity clock goes off in the morning, and you open your eyes to a sound that represents all things positive rather than one that represents danger and fright."

Sheila admitted to Jane she had never thought of it that way. Then she said, "But I don't understand *anything* in my life right now, and calling something an opportunity clock isn't going to solve my problems."

It was now 1:30 p.m., and the time had quickly flown by. It was funny that while Sheila was serving others for the last hour and a half, she hadn't once thought about any of her *own* problems. Compared to the people she had been serving, she realized that maybe her own personal challenges weren't so bad after all. Then she began to doubt herself again.

Tom, the man who had scared her when he came up to the window of her car earlier, approached Jane and proclaimed, "Jane, you know it's my absolute favorite, but that triple-c mac and cheese, with what appeared to be triple bacon, was the best I've ever had. That, along with the stoup—I love how you call it stoup—made for the finest meal I've ever had here. My sincere thanks for improving my day. And that goes for you too, Sheila. Sorry I scared you earlier today by your car."

Sheila paused for a moment, smiled at Tom, and said, "It was a real privilege to serve you today, Tom. Thanks for giving me the opportunity to do so." Jane picked up on it immediately. It may have been slight, but nonetheless it was movement by Sheila in a positive direction.

George, Jane, and Sheila began to clean up. While doing the dishes, Jane wanted to go a little deeper to address Sheila's statement that calling something different than what she normally called it didn't solve her problems. Jane had also remembered that Sheila had earlier asked for "the secret," and it was time to share that Sheila herself had been in possession of it the whole time." We all possess it. It's just that no one ever introduced it to us and taught us how to use it.

"Sheila, what you may have missed when I was describing the difference in perspective regarding a clock was that I was really describing a life tool that can be utilized to positively manage our lives so that we live each day to its fullest. Changing one word can change our entire world. Perspective is one of the most powerful tools we have at our disposal. But it's just like the hammer I described earlier. If you've never been instructed in how to use it and how to maximize its utilization, it's like trying to pound or remove a nail with the handle. It's so hard attempting to use a tool incorrectly that it's easier just to give up and give in. I admit I'm a wishful thinker, but wouldn't it be wonderful if everyone in the world was taught how to utilize perspective at an early age? What if it was one of the core classes that were required in elementary school? You see, having the right perspective not only takes time to learn, *it takes practice.*

"Without perspective practice, you may experience success, but for so many it ends up being *success without fulfillment.* It's exactly where I sense you are right now. What's really cool is that, just like with anything else, the more we practice, the better we get at utilizing perspective as a tool. The goal with perspective is that, with practice, we train our subconscious to respond, rather than react, in a positive way to every area of our life, without even having to think deeply.

Just like my tying-our-shoes example earlier. Practice improves our subconscious mind's ability to take control. Managing our perspective means managing our self-talk and examining the exact wording we use when we chat with ourselves. Whether you think you can, or you think you can't, you're correct.

"Here's a great example, just like the opportunity clock. Substitute the word *have* with the word *get*. Instead of 'I *have* to make dinner,' try saying, 'I *get* to make dinner.' Changing that one word takes your focus from it being a burden to seeing in your mind all of the benefits that occur when you prepare a meal: You satiate hunger; you embrace the opportunity to eat something you like and something that's healthy; you create a social opportunity with people you love; and on and on from a positive perspective. At the end of the day, which perspective will serve you better? The 'I *have* to' or the 'I *get* to' perspective?"

Sheila began to smile as she sensed a transformation happening, all because of the ability to change just one word in a sentence.

"I remember when my mom first went on oxygen," Jane continued. "The first five days were focused on her *having* to wear this tube delivering oxygen for the rest of her life and that her life was ruined. But on day six she awoke with a new perspective, embracing the reality that she *gets* to wear this tube delivering oxygen. She realized that a world she once knew but had lost due to her inability to catch her breath, had now been re-presented to her—all because she changed the word *have* to the word *get*. On day six she spent the entire day creating a list of all the things she could now do because she '*gets*' to wear a tube delivering oxygen, and by the end of the day she had come up with sixty-three things she had previously had to say 'no' to that she could now enjoy again. She could feel fulfilled again. You came here today specifically to be with me because five years ago I was standing in your shoes. I've been given the opportunity to share with you the wisdom of knowing that if you examine the perspective of each thing you're struggling with, you can turn it into one of the most compelling and joyous things in your life. Your focus won't be on success as much as it is on feeling fulfilled. Is it worth a try? Is it worth any effort? I'm proof that it is.

"Look, I'm not proud of where I once was, but I wouldn't be here today had I not hit bottom. I finally realized that I could go no lower than when I consistently sought ways to hurt the people that loved me the most. My husband was, and still is, CEO of a large corporation, and I berated him daily for not focusing more on me, even though he was providing a life for me and our children that most people only dream about. I'd lash out at my kids for not being perfect, even though they always gave everything their very best effort.

"The few friends I had left attempted to help me—help that I told them I didn't need. At least they were frank with me when they informed me that spending time with me had become a painful experience for them. One morning I was in the middle of a mental breakdown while driving my car. I was distracted for a second, jumped a curb, and hit a tree. The airbags deployed and sent me into a state of shock. I wandered into a building right next to the tree to look for help. The moment I stepped into the building, I felt like I was being healed, both mentally and physically. Everything changed for me in that moment. Someone had witnessed my crash, called an ambulance, and saw me stumble into the building, which ended up being—"

"Wait, don't tell me," Sheila interrupted. "The Answer Discovery."

"Right. It's always a miracle when fate intervenes at just the right moment. I was told to meet with George the next day at the homeless shelter. The medical staff at the emergency room would tell my family that I just kept repeating over and over that I had to meet George the next day at the homeless shelter. My family made sure I made it there, and the rest is history. It was George that taught me to focus less on success and more on the joy of fulfillment, simply by changing my perspective and seeing things from a new point of view. Helping others at the homeless shelter provided a wonderful vehicle for me to learn about the benefits that helping others provides. It's funny how people who knew the old me treat me differently now. New people I meet say things that encourage me to continue down the PPP (proper perspective path). With help from George, I decided to leave all of the emptiness and despair behind me and begin anew each day with a perspective based on joy, love, gratitude, peace, and hope. And it works. Like I said earlier, I'm proof that life can improve in an instant, and I'm proof that your life can too. I already have proof that you have an awesome perspective about helping others and putting their needs ahead of your own."

Sheila responded, "You mean by working here today?"

"No!" Jane exclaimed. "I mean by the way you came to the rescue when my dad fell on the sidewalk yesterday."

"That … that was your father?" Sheila asked, trying to put it all together.

"Yes. He's my dad, and he told me that an angel driving a white Mercedes helped ease his embarrassment and bandage his hands after he fell in front of the place he likes to call the New Life Palace. When I saw you pull in, I knew it was you. You know what that means, don't you? It means you have potential you haven't even come close to tapping into for helping others. I saw it right away. Your subconscious is already prepared to make a huge positive difference in the world. The only help you really need is perspective management, perspective practice, and allowing yourself to feel fulfilled. That comes each day with word substitution in any self-talk that leads to a more positive perspective. Just like substituting the word *opportunity* for the word *alarm* when referring to a clock or the word *get* for the word *have* when tasks are right in front of you. That's such a powerful tool, and it's a tool you are already in possession of.

"There's one final tool that I'd like to provide you with. It's a tool you will use anytime you feel yourself slipping back to your old thought processes and perspectives. Slipping back will happen, especially over the next couple of weeks, and this tool will instantly get you back on the path of perspective success. It's actually a saying that my angel gave to me, and it saved me over and over again as I trained my mind to better manage perspective. The saying is: '*When you change the way you look at things, the things you look at change.*'

"So our work here is done for today, and it's time for your gift that you were sent here for. Therefore, Sheila, may I present to you **The Gift of Perspective Management.** Once you have received this gift and learned how to utilize it in your pursuit of the special plan that is yours in life, please share it with others in the following fashion: Begin each day with a self-talk reflecting on the Gift of Perspective Management and the positive role it can play in your life and the lives of all the people you'll encounter that day. Utilize word replacement to alter meanings from negative descriptors to positive descriptors. Utilize the power of repetitive encouragement in your self-talk throughout each day. Repeat until you believe. Repeat and practice until it finds its home in your subconscious. If you slip and find yourself moving backward, pull out the saying, 'When you change the way you look at things, the things you look at change,' and utilize it to immediately bring you back to the desired frame of mind. And remember, *I believe in you,* and I will always be there for you if you need me. Here's my contact information.

"I hope you consider coming back here and helping us prepare some more stoup and triple-c-and-b mac and cheese. It was a privilege spending the last four hours with you, Sheila. Take good care, and thanks again for helping my dad yesterday. I sure appreciate knowing there are lots of angels around him when I'm not there."

With tears of joy in her eyes and a newfound spirit, Sheila embraced Jane in a warm hug and wasn't sure if she wanted to let go. When she did, she softly spoke to Jane, saying, "My word substitution practicing begins right now as I bid you 'good hello' rather than goodbye. I know that 'hello' signifies a beginning with continuation to follow; 'bye' signifies an end and an uncertain future. Thanks to you, and the Gift of Perspective Management, I know that my future is bright, and so I will repeat myself and tell you 'good hello.'"

Jane smiled widely and said, "Good hello, my newfound friend, and thank you for letting me share my perspective today."

Sheila got into her car and knew exactly where she was headed. She was headed home. She had never in her life been so excited to share what had happened to her today with her husband and children. She knew her life had been improved forever, and she wanted to begin practicing her self-talk, word substitution, and perspective management right away. In a single day she had been able to free herself from her self-doubt and negative thinking and had been given a gift that she now wanted to share with anyone willing to listen. She looked forward to the practice every day, knowing that someday the Answer Discovery would be sending her someone whose shoes she had previously walked in.

THE GIFT OF LIVING
LIFE HELPING OTHERS

t was a gorgeous June day in Michigan as Adam swung his car into the empty spot. The small structure to his right, called the Answer Discovery, had been constructed earlier that year in his hometown while he was away at college. The word that perfectly summed up the second semester of his freshman year? *Overwhelming*. At first he thought he was going through culture shock, but he had since framed it in his mind as more of a life shock. He had spent most of the year trying to figure out who he had been, who he currently was, and who he wanted to be. That had been more difficult than his classes, which he had passed in an acceptable fashion.

Just who *did* he want to be? He knew he wanted to find out, and he also knew he could sure use the help of a roadmap to get there. He just didn't know where to find that roadmap. That is, until he heard about the Answer Discovery.

As he exited his car, Adam was hopeful. Life up until this point wasn't bad, but he had always felt that there was a special plan for his life, and he hadn't even come close to figuring out what that special plan was. Although the structure looked like it was constructed completely of glass, Adam couldn't see the interior through it. The Answer Discovery didn't reflect like a mirror either. For whatever reason, the entire structure—almost like an igloo…kind of a dome with a door—seemed to have a radiance about it. Not really radiating light, but sort of a soft glow.

Adam knew what he had come here for and was confident that he was about to pursue his destiny by entering this building, but he couldn't help but notice the glow that was so hard to accurately describe as he walked up to the entrance and opened the door. At that moment, he wondered how many people had gotten all the way to the door and chosen *not* to open it. So close, yet unfulfilled. As he entered, he noticed that the interior dimensions seemed vastly different than what he saw from the outside. Adam's first perception was that he had entered a room that was a perfect circle. No, that wasn't correct. It was more like a perfect half of a sphere with brightness that came from a hidden source. And then the word appeared: WEL-COME. That word faded and more words appeared.

HOW MIGHT I SERVE YOU? The words were not spoken, and Adam couldn't discern how they were manifesting. However, he felt different than he did when he was outside the building—actually very comfortable and at peace all of a sudden. He responded to the question.

"I'm trying to seek my destiny…I think. Or, wait…I'm trying to figure out who I want to be in this vast world of billions of people. Well, to be honest, I think I just want to be happy every day for the rest of my life, and I have absolutely no idea where to start."

More words appeared in front of his eyes. They said, THANK YOU FOR CHOOSING TO ENTER THE ANSWER DISCOVERY TODAY. PLEASE VISIT AND INTERVIEW THOMAS SOLOMON THIS EVENING AT SEVEN O'CLOCK. HE RESIDES AT 1732 CLOVER LANE. HE WILL BE EXPECT-ING YOU. Adam suddenly noticed that he felt good. As he went to exit the Answer Discovery, he felt a lot of emotions surging inside of him as he began to mentally anticipate what waited for him at seven o'clock that night. The sensation he couldn't specifically identify was the power of hope.

. . .

At 6:55 that evening Adam parked on the street in front of the house located at 1732 Clover Lane, wondering what was about to happen. Little did he know that his life was about to change forever.

As Adam exited his car, a voice from the extra-large front porch shouted, "Welcome!" At the same time, a middle-aged man jumped out of a porch swing and quickly approached with an outstretched hand. "My name's Tom Solomon, and I sure am glad to have the privilege of your visit tonight." The man warmly shook Adam's hand with both of his. "I've been giddy all day with anticipation of the opportunity to serve you tonight. So right from the get-go I want to say thank you for making my entire day just a little bit better."

A woman had also jumped up from the porch and was now ready to offer a greeting of her own. "Welcome. I'm Tom's better half, commonly referred to as Linda, and I just want to warmly welcome you to our little bit of heaven here on Clover Lane. Would it be all right if I greet you with a hug rather than a handshake? I already feel like you're family."

After Adam and Linda greeted each other with a lean-in hug, Linda asked Adam to join them on the front porch, where there were several comfortable chairs arranged in a semicircle. As they sat down, a boy and a girl—Adam guessed about seventeen and eight years old, respectively—walked out of the house to the front porch, introduced themselves, and asked him if he would join their parents in drinking a nonalcoholic beverage. Mark, who was actually fifteen years old, spoke.

"We have filtered water, iced tea, sweet tea, fresh lemonade, three types of juice, and several types of soda, including diet and regular. Which would you prefer?"

Adam responded, "I guess I'll try some of that lemonade, please."

Seven-year-old Lizzie politely asked, "Would you prefer a small amount of ice, or lots of ice like our daddy likes it?"

"How about a right in the middle amount of ice, please?" responded Adam.

"We'll be back shortly with your drinks," said Mark, and as they turned to go back inside their father looked over at them and said, "Thank you, kids." Adam saw both children smile and then glance at their father as he sent them a loving wink of his eye.

As soon as Mark and Lizzie entered the house, out popped two more children. Twelve-year-old fraternal twins Margaret and Joseph introduced themselves to Adam and asked him what his favorite snack item was. Adam said, "Oh, anything would be fine, but you really needn't bother just for me."

"It's our pleasure to serve you a snack," said Margaret, "but it would please us most if we could serve you your favorite."

Adam had never really been treated like this and was feeling what at first seemed strange or overwhelmed, but he then decided it felt most like gentle gratitude. Yes, that was it. He was grateful that this family was going out of their way to make him feel so welcome. After a short pause, he responded to the question with, "Well, my favorite snack is popcorn, but anything you offer would be just fine."

Joseph replied, "Oh, we're not shooting for 'just fine'; we're aiming for 'beyond awesome.' We all love popcorn, but typically we make the old-fashioned kind by popping it in a pan and adding real butter and a little salt. Would it be all right if we served you that rather than the microwave kind?"

"I would love to try some of your old-fashioned popcorn," responded Adam, and just like that the twins were off with a zip.

As soon as the twins were through the door, Tom suddenly shouted, "Need a hand?" to a next-door neighbor who had just pulled up with what looked like a brand-new couch sticking out the back of a minivan.

"That'd be great, Superman," the neighbor replied. Tom glanced at Adam and said, "Perfect timing. Let's go help out my buddy next door." He then opened the front door and hollered for Mark to help, who was only a few feet away returning to the front porch with Lizzie. They had drinks for their parents and Adam, which they set on a centered table. Then Mark and Adam followed Tom as they approached the neighbor. Tom introduced Adam to his neighbor as a young college student. As they moved the new couch inside, the neighbor got an idea.

"Hey, as a young college kid, I'll bet you could utilize a lightly used couch next year at school." He continued, "My wife is an interior designer, and we're always changing our look. I even have a matching chair that I could give you, and both are only three years old and lightly used. All for free. What do you say?"

Adam almost felt overwhelmed by this generosity and, after a short silence, replied, "That'd be great, if you're sure."

"If you're a friend of Tom's, it'd make me awful happy to know you'll be giving them a home where they'll be enjoyed," the neighbor responded. "Heck, I'll even store them for you in our garage until you're ready to go back to school next semester." Adam couldn't believe that someone whom he had never met until just minutes ago was willing to give him what appeared to be well-built, almost new furniture. What a wonderful gift.

The popcorn was just coming out the front door as they hopped back onto Tom's front porch. Tom, his wife, and all their children were now seated in the semi-circle, along with Adam. Tom could see by the look on Adam's face that he was still processing what had just happened. Tom smiled and said, "Adam, you just experienced, firsthand, *the gift of living life helping others.* That's why you're here tonight." Tom continued, "As a family, we're approaching each day living life helping others whenever an opportunity presents itself. We also look for ways to create opportunities to help others that may not normally be noticed. We attempt, each day, to maintain that mindset until our heads hit our pillows at night. We believe that helping others results in helping ourselves in every area of our life. This way of life has worked very well for our family. May I share with you how we came to embrace this simple gift?"

"Wow…Yes, please…I mean, you and the rest of your family all seem so at peace…or happy…or content…or maybe confident in who you are. I would love to hear your story," stated Adam. And so Tom began.

"Well, it all started back in college when I was between my freshman and sophomore years, just where you are at right now. Though I was doing well in school, I was struggling trying to figure out the 'meaning of life' thing and where I fit into the picture. I had seen things and experienced people that I had never been exposed to before. I spent my entire freshman year analyzing what different people did, how they treated others, how they were treated in return, why some people were liked by what seemed like everyone, and why some didn't seem to get along well with others. I sought out people who seemed to be consistently happy and observed what I could of their daily living habits. I also noticed that people seemed to trend into what I'll call 'like kind' groups. You know, the 'birds of a feather flock together' theory.

"It became apparent to me that people lived up to the expectations, be they good or bad, of the group of people they surrounded themselves with and that there was a natural attraction of 'common thought' or 'common philosophy' that bonded these groups together. In trying to figure out who I wanted to be in life, I thought that the best thing for me was to attempt to get along with *everyone* without necessarily embracing any habits or philosophies that I felt would have even the slightest negative impact on my life. So that summer I devised a plan that had at its core a simple statement: No matter what, I wasn't going to give anyone any reason to view me, nor anything about me, from a negative standpoint.

"At this point I need to 'explain' you down a side road before I return you to the highway. While I had wonderful parents, they were not immersed in their five children's personal and character development. When I went off to college, I didn't possess any real leadership skills or self-esteem. At that time, I also didn't comprehend the role that going to college was supposed to have in a person's life. I ended up focusing on who I wanted to become rather than acquiring a degree that would serve a purpose for the rest of my life. Most of my friends ended up graduating and scoring jobs worthy of their degrees. At that time I was bound and determined to utilize my 'self-realization degree' in resisting a victim mentality of why everyone might be getting ahead of me in life. Now, back to the story.

"Someone I had recently met and had begun a friendship with was a guy named Dan. He unknowingly provided me with the perfect test for my newly devised plan. Dan had been married about a year and a half, and I had been asked to join Dan and his wife Louisa for dinner one night at their apartment. I had yet to meet Louisa, but Dan had told me a fair amount about her, and he shared with me that he had told her a fair amount about me and our growing friendship. I spent a lot of time preparing for that dinner and tried to put myself in Louisa's shoes. I knew that I could possibly present a threat to Louisa—in other words, someone that she would have to compete against for her husband's time in the future. That was not good. I needed to remove that threat from her mind right from the moment she met me. I wanted Louisa to perceive me, and my friendship with Dan, as an asset in her husband's life—one that would support, and even enhance, the foundation of what made their marriage work so well. I had decided that long-term friendship success with Dan, and subsequently Louisa, depended on me focusing on what would make *them* happy. And if *they* were happy, then that would make *me* happy. Win-win-win.

"I love win-win-win. So here's how I approached that dinner: I called Dan the day before and asked him what type of inexpensive flowers I could bring, and he suggested that Louisa liked daisies. So the first time I met Dan's wife, I showed up with daisies. That went over well. They were inexpensive but nice and showed that I had cared enough to take the time to arrive with a thoughtful gift. Next, I proceeded to look and listen for anything that I could make a sincere positive statement about that Louisa would appreciate. I made simple and gentle comments about how their apartment was decorated, how nice the hors d'oeuvres were, how much I appreciated the food she had prepared and served for dinner and dessert, how much I appreciated the time I got to spend with her husband, and how that time was having a positive impact on my life. When we were finished with dinner, I politely insisted on helping clean the dishes. They didn't have an automatic dishwasher back then, and cleaning up after a meal took time. Louisa tried to tell me 'no,' but I was persistent. As Louisa relented, it appeared that she really appreciated the fact that I was helping her rather than sitting out in the living room talking with Dan and ignoring her as she worked on the task at hand. Dan helped too, and the three of us enjoyed the task as interaction and dialogue ensued. I believe that it was the decision to help with the dishes that made Louisa believe that my friendship with Dan would prove to be a win-win-win."

"Then what happened?" Adam inquired. Tom continued:

"I realized that I was onto something with this theory and decided that I would continue to practice and refine it in preparation for my sophomore year back at school. It seemed that no matter where I went, when I encountered any person and didn't give them any reason not to like me, people responded to me in some sort of a positive manner. When people responded to me in a positive manner, it would result in this immediate and long-lasting feeling of joy inside of me. Many years later in life, I would learn that what I was experiencing was a naturally occurring release of serotonin in my body. Serotonin is something our body can produce, based on the right set of circumstances, which makes us happy, joyful, and peaceful.

"After about a month of practicing this theory, I realized that a change had occurred in me without me really noticing it. I was happier each day than I had ever been before, and people seemed to be treating me better than I had ever been treated. I was helping others by doing things for people like holding doors, warmly smiling when our eyes met, paying for the person's order behind me in the drive-thru coffee line, answering the phone with 'good morning' or 'good afternoon' or 'good evening' rather than the standard 'hello,' and volunteering at a wide variety of places that I had never volunteered at before.

"I became more sensitive to other people's immediate needs. I would let a young mother with a fussy baby step in front of me in a checkout line, or help someone who was too short to reach something on the top shelf of the grocery store. I developed the habit of never walking by something that was on the floor or ground that didn't belong there. It may have been a clothing item that had fallen off the rack in a store, a piece of trash that didn't find its way to the trash container, or a box that had fallen off a shelf. It became sort of a 'Do the right thing, no matter what' kind of life, and I absolutely loved it. Was my system perfect? No. But it never failed because I learned that failure never occurs until someone gives up ... and I never gave up. I learned from my missteps, tweaked my approach, and pursued the improved path.

"My life really grew during my sophomore year, and I found myself having access to the type of people that I wanted to surround myself with because of this new philosophy of not giving anyone any reason to dislike me and living life helping others. Look, I know this all sounds weird, but the truth is that it was working really well. My peer group was forming itself, and I found myself living up to the higher expectations that this new peer group held up for me.

As I continued living each day not giving anyone a reason *not* to like me, I realized that what the strategy had morphed into was an attempt to help other people in every situation that presented itself. As time continued, I found that this 'living life helping others' attitude worked well for me in every area of my life, whether it was nurturing friendships, relationships, or even finding employment. It also led me to the most important person and influence in my life: my wonderful wife.

"The truth is that after four and a half years of college, I left without a degree but received something that turned out to be much more influential in determining my path to success in life. That something was high self-esteem, self-confidence, and a deeper understanding of the power of relationships. It provided me with more motivation to succeed than a degree would have. It also has been the primary driver in the way we've chosen to pursue our careers and raise our children. This gift is the foundation of our life, and we are grateful that I somehow stumbled upon it when I was in college. It is a gift that I've been instructed to share with you tonight. That's why you're here. Therefore, Adam, may I present to you **The Gift of Living Life Helping Others**. Once you have received this gift and learned how to utilize it in your pursuit of the special plan that is yours in life, please share it with others in the following fashion:

"Every waking moment of every single day, utilize the gift of living life helping others. Begin with the people you encounter first each morning. If you're with family, begin the day by helping your parents and siblings. If you're married, begin the day by helping your spouse. If you're a father or mother, begin by being a helper, first to your spouse, and then to your children. These are the people that begin your day. Then transition into the next group. Typically that would be the other community members you encounter on the roads you select as you drive to work. You serve and help them by being courteous and thoughtful. Next may be your coworkers. Let your work support *their* efforts and dreams. Help them by leading when leadership opportunities present themselves and by following when you have an opportunity to support their lead. Inspire rather than motivate, and supportively mentor when you have experience that others don't. Continue your day with a smile at every personal encounter and develop a greeting that goes beyond hello. Praise all good work and show gratitude with what you do and say. Helping others requires knowledge of their interests and goals, so seek to understand where they want to go in life and what their plan is for getting there. Then develop strategies that allow you to best help them reach their dreams.

"Finish each day with the people you're closest to, just as you began the day, serving their needs and making sure that they grew in a positive manner in some area of their life that day. Always keep in mind that helping and serving *oneself* is nothing more than selfishness. Selfish people die unfulfilled, because 'enough' is never actually enough. Living the Gift of Living Life Helping Others is the opposite of selfishness. The reward of *selflessness* is living a fulfilling and wonderful life each and every day."

Adam was silent for a moment. Finally, he said, "Wow, I feel a little overwhelmed, but at the same time I feel like you've given me a great gift by allowing me to visit with you and your family. Here's the question that's swirling around in my mind right now: What am I supposed to do now?"

Tom responded, "Well that's exactly the right question, and the great news is that *you* get to determine the answer. When I was informed that you would be visiting, I was also informed that I would be giving you a seed. Not a physical seed per se, but the sharing of my knowledge and wisdom that I have experienced in life. You now have that seed, and what you do with it is entirely up to you. Please know that we as a family will be cheering for you always as you pursue the incredible path of your future."

Adam accepted the second bowl of popcorn that was offered and quietly observed the banter going on within this unique family. He knew that his life was about to change—no, *improve*—and he couldn't wait to begin. He asked if he could come back frequently over the summer to fine-tune the lessons he had just learned. It was Linda who confirmed that it was a requirement, because from now on, Adam was just like family to all of them.

THE GIFT OF RELATIONSHIPS

What an incredible day it was. To begin with, it was Saturday. You'd be hard-pressed to find anyone who wouldn't consider Saturday their favorite day of the week. It just offered so many different opportunities and possibilities. Plus, for most individuals who work Monday through Friday, no one owns a piece of their time on Saturdays. Saturday represents complete freedom—freedom from all of life's responsibilities—at least for a day.

Caren's mind was about to go down the path of attempting to discern how many in our current society viewed Sundays in the same way as Saturdays, but she resisted the urge to mimic a dog seeing a squirrel by having her focus take a ninety-degree turn. Thanks to her parents naming her Caren with a "C" rather than a "K," she had become a professional at deflecting distraction. Funny how her mom and dad felt so strongly about naming her when she was born.

They had put a lot of time into coming up with a name that signified their hopes that she would grow up to be someone who cared about *everything*, just like they did. Caren had learned to accept that when they used her name, they called her Care, leaving off the "n" and allowing people to think they were just using a shortened version of Karen. She also acknowledged that the spelling confused some people attempting to pronounce it, and she often heard Caren pronounced like Lauren or Car-in.

None of it mattered anymore once she was past high school because by then, every time someone found out how she spelled her name or mispronounced it, she had trained herself to immediately think of the genuine love her parents had for her, how willing they were to totally believe in her, how they supported all the decisions she made in life, and how much they *cared* for her. It was a foundation that not everyone else had and one that she hoped she could help establish in the people entrusted to her care.

What a privilege it was for her to be a professor at one of the most respected business schools in the country! It's precisely what was inspiring the mission she was on today. She knew what she wanted, and she just needed help obtaining the absolute best fit. When someone had asked her recently what one of her personal superpowers was, she had responded that it was her ability to be present in the moment in all of her life experiences. And she was certainly present in the moment when she pulled into the vacant parking space in front of the Answer Discovery.

It seemed that being present in the moment allowed her to draw more pleasure from each experience than most other people achieved. She had acquired the skill from spending a lot of time with a person who had taught her many life lessons. His name was Jon Barckholtz, and he had moved on to Heaven just three short months ago, at the tender age of fifty-three. Their friendship had begun fifteen years ago when Caren walked up behind Jon's wheelchair at a potluck dinner line and offered to help him get his food and get seated. They were both being elected that night to the board of the local Arc chapter, an advocate group for people with intellectual and developmental disabilities. Caren had a brother two years older than her who was autistic and noncommunicative. He loved Caren more than anyone else on this earth, including their parents, and Caren experienced a unique display of love from her brother on a daily basis. Her brother was the reason she was nominated to the Arc board of directors, and she credited him for providing the opportunity for her to meet Jon Barckholtz. Her life changed forever with the relationship that began at that potluck. Over the ensuing fifteen years, Jon would teach Caren many lessons in life that only a person who had experienced a life like Jon's could know.

Jon's journey on this earth did not start out on a path that would typically produce such a happy, positive person. Born with spina bifida, he spent his first twenty years of life at a state institution. There, he endured abuse, neglect, the loss of a leg, and a sense of loneliness that could have left him broken and hopeless. Instead, he successfully dedicated his adult life to ensuring that others would never have to be separated from family and community again. Jon had developed several perspectives that were "lifelong winners," and he loved sharing those perspectives with anyone who would listen. Over the fifteen years they knew each other, Jon had become Caren's best friend, and she treasured all that Jon had taught her.

After parking, Caren turned the vehicle off and went into the sixty-second trance that would help her prepare to mentally record what was about to happen next. Doing this would allow her to pull this memory from her mental file cabinet decades later and be able to share the details of what transpired. She closed her eyes, controlled her breathing, and, once fully prepared to be present in the moment, she exited her vehicle, briskly walked up to the door of the building, and stepped inside.

As much as she had prepared for this moment, she couldn't help but feast her eyes on the beauty of the interior she had just stepped into. She allowed it to gently sink in as she began to record the experience with her mind's eye. After about three minutes of silence, her mind heard, WELCOME, CAREN WITH A 'C.' IT'S GREATLY APPRECIATED THAT YOU'RE PRESENT IN THE MOMENT. LIFE IS FULL OF PRECIOUS MOMENTS THAT CAN BE FILED IN OUR MEMORY BANKS FOR FUTURE USE AND EMBRACEMENT. HOW CAN THE ANSWER DISCOVERY SERVE YOU ON THIS GLORIOUS SATURDAY?

Caren responded, "Wonderful morning. I'm a business professor at the local university. One of the life lessons I've developed, with the help of my best friend, who recently passed away, is developing and utilizing the power of relationships. I'd like to introduce this life lesson to my current students, but I keep running into a mental roadblock in developing a lesson that begins with a powerful message that will immediately get my students' attention, and will also have a lasting, positive impact on them for the rest of their lives. Would you have an answer that will help me with this challenge?"

Caren immediately sensed the answer. HAVE YOUR 1:00–2:30 P.M. CLASS READY FOR A GUEST SPEAKER THIS WEDNESDAY. HIS NAME IS GEORGE, AND HE'LL ARRIVE JUST BEFORE CLASS BEGINS WITH AN OUTLINE OF HIS LESSON ENTITLED 'RELATIONSHIPS AND THEIR IMPACT ON YOUR LIFE.' YOU'LL WANT TO VIDEOTAPE HIS PRESENTATION, WHICH HE'LL GIVE YOU WRITTEN PERMISSION TO UTILIZE AT YOUR WILL IN THE FUTURE. ENJOY THE REST OF THIS GLORIOUS SATURDAY MORNING, CAREN WITH A 'C.' IT'S AN HONOR TO SERVE YOU.

Caren heard herself speak the words, "Thank you so very much!" but she sensed that the building she was about to exit could sense her extreme gratitude as she made her final pause to record in her mind what had just occurred.

Each day following that Saturday felt like a week as the excitement within her kept building. She had tried to be patient, waiting for Wednesday to arrive, and it finally had. At noon Caren was pausing to prepare her mind to draw the maximum amount of pleasure and recall from the presentation by a mystery man named George.

She had to practice distraction deflection again, with her mind asking questions like, *Who is this man named George? What does he do for a living? Is it business-related? How will he outline what he's going to present? How will it impact the students today? Will it provide fundamental principles that my students can add to their life foundation and move them toward success in life, regardless of their profession?* That was her dream, of course. She closed her eyes, took some deep breaths, and was able to reduce her heart rate as she kept repeating to herself, "Be calm. Be in the moment. Draw pleasure from the experience. Mark it in your mind."

It was now 12:45 p.m., and students began to file into the auditorium-style classroom. Caren had asked them to arrive early if they could, so that they would all be present and ready by the time one o'clock rolled around. While Caren wondered how the man named George would know which classroom was hers, she had faith from her visit to the Answer Discovery that he could find his way without her help.

 · · ·

At precisely 12:55, George entered the room and walked toward Caren with what appeared to be an outline in his hand. Caren glanced up and immediately recognized him. Having been given no other clue than his first name, she never would have anticipated that the George heading toward her was, in fact, the CEO of a Fortune 50 company located about two hours from their community. While she had successfully placed about two dozen of her graduates with this worldwide leader in their industry, she realized that she was experiencing a dream she never thought to dream. It had always seemed like too big of an ask, and yet here he was: George Dasina.

By then her students were all present, and they were beginning to settle down as word started spreading among them about who this man who would be speaking to them today was. George introduced himself to Caren and requested that she not introduce him. He just wanted to begin right at one o'clock with a short story that would lead to his casual, conversational presentation. Everything he would cover was in the outline he handed her, along with a signed slip allowing her to utilize all of what he planned to present. He was glad she was videotaping and requested that she send him a copy of the presentation, if possible, so he could utilize it to improve his presentation style. Caren was more than happy to comply with his requests.

At 12:59 George paused as he was looking directly at Caren and said, "I have one last request. Would you be willing to devote some time to me in the future, allowing us to further develop a professional relationship? I've done some research on you and really feel that you have some skill sets that I could learn from, and in turn I could apply some of my life experiences in an effort to help you. Would that work?"

Caren smiled and replied, "That would be wonderful!"

They exchanged business cards, and they both laughed when they realized that, prior to meeting each other, both of them had added their cell phone numbers on the back of their business cards. The first thought that came to both their minds was, "Great minds think alike." Then Caren seated herself off to the side of the podium, and George looked out at the eager faces in front of him and began speaking.

"If there were a way for you to compress decades of learning from your own experiences into days of learning from *other* people's experiences, you'd want to know about it, wouldn't you? The reason for asking is that I was taught a way to do precisely that, and I'd like to share the system I've discovered. It's based on one word, and that word is *relationships*.

"I'm here to share with you what I have learned about the power of relationships and how they can be the most important tool in your 'toolbox for life.' Now I just used the term *toolbox for life* because this particular tool, and the impact it can have, is designed, not only for your career life, but for *every single aspect* of life you will experience. I'll define the tool and explain why it's so important to each of your lives. I'll also teach you why you should never abuse the tool, which can render it useless and inflict pain when mistreated.

"My dad was a successful small business entrepreneur. He made his living in the dry-cleaning industry. His industry, along with five other related industries, had a convention and trade show every two years. When I was seventeen, my dad informed one of my younger brothers and me that we would accompany him for a week in Atlanta, Georgia, at this massive trade show. On the flight to Atlanta, our dad coached us in preparation for the show. He had developed a plan. A side note here: Both of our parents *loved* developing a plan and then executing that plan for everything our family did.

"Back to the plan, which he had dubbed the 'Flight Plan' based on the timing of him presenting it to us. My brother and I just thought he was weird at the time and kind of half chuckled. The plan he had created for the week was for us to remain focused—for the entire week—on one word. The word was *relationships*, and the entire trip would revolve around us gaining a deep understanding of this word and the role it could play in our lives. He explained that, through relationships, we could hyper-accelerate our learning of principles and life tools, while being able to share with others different lessons we had learned that they hadn't yet. The goal was always to obtain, nurture, and grow a win-win relationship that led to spectacular outcomes for both parties. Our dad had been including us on business trips, seminars, and important meetings with his banker, CPA, attorney, and insurance agent from the time we were ten. We had grown to be excited about our dad's plans because they always turned out to be an adventure. So we were eager to see how he would execute the plan he had developed around the word *relationships*.

"Dad began by asking if we had noticed how he treated the person at the airline ticket counter, the TSA workers as we came through their line, the people we encountered at the gate waiting to board just like us, those who helped us board the plane, the stewardess who welcomed us on the plane, the pilots as we passed by the cockpit, the people we passed as we located our seats, and the people who were seated around us. As our dad was asking us this, my brother and I realized that we had been more focused on the excitement of traveling, which we loved, than on the specifics of my dad's actions. Dad knew that too but was setting the stage. From this point on during the trip, we would observe Dad with every person he encountered, and then we would discuss the interaction afterward to draw conclusions from our observations.

"When we arrived in Atlanta, we caught a taxi to our hotel and checked into the room that would be home for the three of us for the next week. As soon as we unpacked and got organized, Dad started the questions. Did we notice how he treated the taxi driver? Was he respectful to the driver? Had we learned anything about the driver's personal life? About his family? Did we know how long he had been at his present job? Did we know what he liked best about his job and what he would change if we gave him a magic wand? Had the driver asked us any questions? What had he learned about us? Did he offer anything unique to us, utilizing his knowledge of Atlanta, that he thought we would enjoy?

"Dad was always refining his relationship development process, and we became fascinated with watching him. We cleaned up and went down to the hotel's restaurant for dinner. We had run into a longtime industry friend of Dad's, and he had asked if she and her husband would like to join us for dinner. When the five of us arrived together at the entrance to the restaurant, a hostess greeted us and asked how many would be dining.

"Before our dad gave a number, he complimented the hostess on her smile and shared how he felt that she was in a perfect job to take full advantage of that million-dollar smile. He revealed how powerful a warm, inviting smile was for people traveling far from home. He thanked her for making us all feel so welcome and told her how fortunate we were for having *her* be our hostess tonight. Once the five of us were seated, and before we could discuss the impact of all he had said to the hostess, our dad began the process again with the waiter. We were seated in the middle of the restaurant, and the waiter taking care of us was also responsible for the five tables surrounding us. We were able to observe how he was treating the other tables and compare that to our own experience, based on how Dad would engage with him and how the other tables engaged with him. We learned so much from this comparative analysis. Dad always seemed to make it fun, and my brother and I were having a blast while learning some valuable lessons. We also watched him manage his relationship with his longtime friend and her husband.

"Later, when the three of us were back in our hotel room, we reviewed all that had happened that day. We looked at the results of each experience, from the time we arrived at the departing airport to the time we came up to our room. My brother and I were quick to agree that every single experience that day seemed to be at least a little better than that of the people around us sharing the same environment. We went into deep discussion as to why we thought this occurred. We concluded that the sincere personal interest that our father offered to each person we became engaged with that day had paid us big dividends.

"Amazingly, with our dad, it was never huge or overblown interest, nor did he overstep any social boundaries. He just offered a warm smile, admiration for something he noticed about the individual, and sincere good wishes. What amazed us most was the innate ability our father had to notice something good about anyone and everyone. He could turn nearly anything into an instant asset, and he began many conversations complimenting people for whatever that asset happened to be. A smile, loving eyes, beautiful hair, colors of clothes that looked good, nice shoes, sleek cell phone or computer, and more. He'd notice sports teams and colleges displayed on shirts and hats and could pepper an individual with questions for over an hour, gaining huge amounts of knowledge and information while listening to someone who had a lot of passion for the school, team, state, country, religion, industry, or issue they were talking about and promoting on what they were wearing.

"Dad knew that everyone cared about something, and everyone had something about themselves that they really liked. He was always curious about what that was. The rest of the week in Atlanta exposed us to a wide variety of relationships our dad embraced, from meeting someone for the first time to advancing the relationship with people he knew previously. We learned many things on that trip to Atlanta. Things like treating others with kindness always enhanced an interaction. Sincerely complimenting someone always resulted in a better experience. Being interested in other people's lives rather than trying to tell them all about yours helped you grow as a human being and offered the probability of a trusted relationship that could grow. Asking the right questions opened people's desire to share their knowledge with you. Usage of phrases and questions like, *Tell me more,* and, *What led you to that?* and, *Why is that so important to you?* really helped to move relationships in a positive direction.

"So why did I begin with a story about a trip to Atlanta when I was seventeen? Because the things I learned about relationships on that trip became an important part of the success I've enjoyed in all of the areas of my life. The timing was also great, as it was right before I went to college. While in college, I put the power of relationships to work right away with several of my professors. I received help and support from them that impacted internships I landed during the summers of my collegiate career. Several of them recommended me for leadership positions on campus and as a representative of the university for several conferences around the U.S., which placed me in the presence of many business and political leaders in the country.

"Those professor relationships led to advice on pursuing specific companies upon graduation and assessing whether I wanted to transition right into an MBA program or if I should get a couple years of experience under my belt. The choices I made leaned heavily on those relationships, just like the choices and decisions I've made since then and continue to make, including being here with all of you today. Let me dive a little deeper into the 'relationships' thought process.

"During an interview for a news article, I was asked about the role relationships have played in my life. I smiled because I'm not sure the interviewer was ready for my response. I began by telling them that every successful relationship is built upon trust. Nothing is more important for the ongoing success of any relationship than trust, whether it's a marriage, a business relationship, a friendship, or the purchase of goods or services. Trust can be won or lost in a second.

"I gave a couple of examples. First, one day I was inadvertently playing the role of an idiot when I was walking down a busy city sidewalk while texting. I was about to step off the curb into oncoming traffic when a woman grabbed my coat from behind and gave me a yank that nearly popped me out of my shoes. Realizing she had just most likely saved my life, it took less than a second for me to trust her—a complete stranger—at the highest level possible. We're now close friends.

"The second story is about how, in my mid-thirties, I broke my neck ice skating while trying to 'zing' one of my brothers. I knew I was in trouble when the emergency room doctor informed me that if they didn't perform emergency surgery to rebuild my neck that very day, I would end up a quadriplegic. Unfortunately, it was a Sunday, and they would have to make some calls to bring in the team needed to perform the necessary surgery. Never had the ability to quickly develop relationships of complete trust with the people they were calling in on their day off been more important to my life.

"Three hours later, when everyone who would be part of putting my crushed neck back together had arrived, I requested two minutes to address all of them. In those two minutes I thanked them for showing up, told them that I trusted 100 percent the skills and abilities that made each of them unique, and asked them to trust that, when I recovered from the successful surgery they were about to perform, I would utilize my restored health to help others to the best of my ability. I had requested instant trust between all of us, and, based on me standing in front of you today, as healthy as can be, it obviously worked.

"An example of trust being *lost* in a second is when an executive at our very own company fabricated a story about an individual that worked for a competitor in an attempt to eliminate that competitor from a business opportunity we were both bidding on. When I found out about the fabrication, *all* trust was lost in this individual. It was an action from which there was no possibility of recovery. They were immediately fired, and their actions resulted in us being eliminated from consideration for work that would have employed hundreds of additional people.

"The interviewer for the article appreciated the stories I had shared and, before leaving, I said, 'When you think about it, relationships and the trust that those relationships command, in one way or another, are responsible for the foundation of every decision we make in life.' It was that sentence that became the headline of the article that appeared in the paper the next day.

"My goal today, in the hour I was given, is to give you the *why* of how relationships are so important in every area of your life. I've left additional information with your professor for any of you that are interested in learning the *how* of initiating, nurturing, growing, and embracing the role relationships will play as you advance through life. I'd like to finish with a couple of short stories that will allow you to view relationships from some additional perspectives than those I've described so far. They'll give you both the *why* and the *how*. One describes the ultimate benefits of a life built around relationships, and the other shares how my wife and I have been creative in teaching our children about the gift of relationships.

"On a recent trip with some of our executive team, the discussion turned to how each of us would be remembered when we died. It immediately took me back to an incredible book I read by Stephen R. Covey entitled *The 7 Habits of Highly Effective People*. The habit that had the greatest impact on my life was the second one: 'Begin with the end in mind.' The habit placed us, invisibly, at our own funeral, where four people would be speaking—one from each of the following groups: family, friends, coworkers, and community. The question the exercise begged was, *What would they say?* For me personally, as I pondered what people from those four groups would say about me, it begged the question, *Who determines what they will say?* I have come to fully believe and embrace that each and every one of us has complete control over what they will say about us at our funeral. The words they speak at our funeral will describe our character that they came to intimately know through the relationship we had with them.

"As we nurture and grow a relationship, we have an opportunity to share our true character through our words and actions. If we take time to think about what we would like anyone to say about us in the future, it means we're always focused on doing what's right rather than what may seem best at the moment. It's the long-term view versus the short-term 'one and done' view. Through always attempting to do the right thing, we develop what I like to call a 'consistency of character' that shapes the thoughts and words of others and how we'll be remembered.

"I further realized that, if you want to have any chance of developing powerful relationships in your life, you have to manage your personal character in every relationship you develop. The things we do today will determine what people think of us tomorrow and beyond. Are you managing everything you say, all of your actions, and everything you post on the internet on this day to achieve the results of how people will describe you tomorrow? It can be a powerful, life-changing process, should you decide to embrace it, and also the very first step to developing deep, win-win relationships that will make your life, and the life of many others, better.

"I decided to take this life principle a step further after attending a lecture by an author and gifted speaker named Brian Molitor. In that lecture, Brian shared a thought process that improved my words and actions. He said,

'Imagine that a new neighbor moves into a house on your street, and you go down to introduce yourself and welcome them to the street. If they ask you, "Where are you from?" and you respond by pointing at a house two down from theirs on the opposite side and say, "The house with the yellow siding," *instantly* you represent every other person that resides in your house. If you're kind of a jerk and let this brand-new neighbor know that your family takes pride in keeping your grass perfectly cut and your yard perfectly landscaped and then suggest that they should too … well, from that point forward they will believe that everyone *else* that lives in your house must *also* be a jerk.

"At the same time, if you present yourself as a kind and caring person, handing them some fresh-baked cookies, welcoming them to the street, letting them know if they ever need anything they can count on you, and that you love helping other people whenever an opportunity presents itself… well, from that point forward they will believe that everyone *else* that lives in your house must *also* be a kind and caring individual.

'In that moment everyone who resides in your home is being judged and represented by *you*. The same applies in every situation where you find yourself interacting with others. When you meet someone who's moving to your community and they ask, "Where are you from?" and you respond by saying, "The Valley Hills neighborhood, right near the library," *instantly* you represent the more than two hundred and fifty people living in the hundred or so homes in your neighborhood. When you're out of town and meet someone who asks you, "Where are you from?" and you respond by saying, "Crystal Blue, near the center of the state," *instantly* you represent the more than fifty-three thousand people who live in your city.

'When you travel out of state and someone asks you, "Where are you from?" and you respond by saying, "Michigan," *instantly* you represent a total of nearly ten million people. The same holds true for when you travel outside the United States and someone asks you, "Where are you from?" and you respond by saying, "The United States," *instantly* you represent over 330 *million* people.'

"Then Brian paused long enough for all of us to be just this side of uncomfortable and asked those of us attending, 'Why do people in France hate people in the United States so much? They used to love us. They admired us so much they gave us the Statue of Liberty as a gift. We saved their rear ends during World War II. If it wasn't for the U.S., they wouldn't even exist as a country right now. Could it be that individuals from the United States interacted with the French and represented all of us horribly?'

"Brian's presentation had a huge impact on me and how I interpreted the flow of relationships. I realized people create their own thoughts about groups, large and small, based on what they're experiencing with the individual right in front of them. It's really a perfect example of what math calls the transitive property of equality. Do you all remember the property that states if A=B and B=C, then A=C? Brian helped me realize that if jerk=you, and you=the only person a French citizen has ever met from the United States, then jerk=United States. It also works the other way. If awesome, kind, compassionate, and loving=you, and you=the only person a French citizen has ever met from the United States, then awesome, kind, compassionate, and loving=United States.

"Well, over 99 percent of the people I have interacted with in the United States are *wonderful* people. Someday, I hope I have an opportunity to present the United States to the entire population of France as I have come to know it. In the meantime, we're missing out on what could be a wonderful relationship with France as trusted, appreciated, and respected allies. So I want to reduce it down to the level that most of us live with every day of our lives and the number of people we may be impacting with our personal actions.

"Think about this: when someone asks me what church I attend, *at that moment and to that person* I'm representing everyone that belongs to our parish. If someone finds out I'm an active Rotarian, *at that moment and to that person* I'm representing Rotarians worldwide. If someone finds out we have a son with disabilities, then *at that moment and to that person*, I'm representing all families that have a child with disabilities. And on and on it goes. It clicked in my mind, and I further realized that everything I say, all of my actions, and everything I post on the internet ... it all matters. Not just to me, but to everyone I represent with every interaction I have. If I'm being interviewed on a televised program as the CEO of a Fortune 50 company and that interview will be posted on the internet, I'm representing more than 115,000 of the worldwide teammates from our company. All of this led me to carefully and intentionally manage my thoughts, words, actions, and character. It was the successful management of those four things that led me to the ability to quickly create a high level of trust with another individual and accelerate the relationship process.

"Shortly after hearing Brian speak and playing around with what he had taught me and the additional processes that led to, I wanted to test some of my new realizations out. The most willing volunteers who wouldn't know they were being used as guinea pigs were my wife and kids. The best way to experiment would be lengthy discussions followed up by practical usage of the theories I wanted to test. And the best way to accomplish that? A road trip!

"Like many couples living in the Midwest, my wife and I had always talked about renting a motor home and heading west. So one day we decided we *were actually going to commit to doing it* with our four kids ... and we did. We left the rental RV dealer in southwest Michigan at about two o'clock on the beautiful afternoon of June 28. We had three great days of traveling, stopping at some wonderful historic sites along the way. The six of us traveling in a motor home allowed for deep discussions in a comfortable environment. It also allowed us to stop at some unique places each night and try out what we had discussed earlier while driving. We finally arrived at a KOA campground in Cody, Wyoming, on July 1. For the next four days we explored Yellowstone National Park. It was wonderful, and I could share stories for days about the beauty of what we saw. What I really want to share is how we began each morning as a family at the campground.

"You see, when you stay at this particular KOA campground, your site rental includes all the pancakes you care to enjoy, along with juice or fresh-brewed coffee from 7 to 10 a.m. each morning. If you were so inclined, you could purchase three sausage links for two dollars. Because it was included in the site rental, nearly everyone staying there took advantage of the 'free pancakes and coffee or juice' offer. This led to having to wait in line for the pancakes that were being prepared. It gave me time to observe the one person responsible for cooking the pancakes.

"She stood over a hot griddle that was thirty inches wide by six feet long. You could just sense that she had mastered her responsibilities and was in control, just like a high-wire walker without the use of a net. Others helped with keeping plates, utensils, coffee cups, butter, and syrup at the ready, but the pancakes were the sole responsibility of Marge, and you could tell that Marge prepared each and every pancake with a huge dose of love. Every once in a while, she'd look down the line and, if she spotted someone under the age of ten, she'd create an unusual artistic pancake in the shape of an animal, bird, or shark and serve it up with a huge smile.

"In fact, she even served the good old round ones up with that million-dollar smile she had. She shared the smile and the pancakes with everyone from the campers who were staying in motor homes that must have cost several hundred thousand dollars to those camping in older tents that allowed them to see the stars through holes in the top that hadn't been patched yet. It didn't matter to Marge. She appeared to have enough joy to spread around to everyone. And her pancakes weren't just good; they were *exceptional*.

"On the third day I inquired where she purchased her pancake mix and told her how much I enjoyed the pancakes. She smiled and replied that the mix was her own recipe, one that her grandmother had passed down to her. When I mentioned that I could identify that one of the ingredients seemed to be love, she responded that her grandma had told her that love was the most important ingredient in *any* recipe. I couldn't help but smile and agree with her.

"When our fifth and final morning at the campground arrived, we cleaned up early and went over to have our last breakfast. It was wonderful and brought us great joy to begin our day once more, just as we had the previous four. We went back, started cleaning up our campsite, and began to load up to get back on the road. It was about 9:50 a.m., and I knew breakfast was winding down for the day. As my wife kept packing and putting things in the proper place for our next stop, I gathered the boys, told them they were about to learn a great lesson about life, and had them follow me to the covered outdoor area where breakfast was served.

"When we arrived, there were only about a dozen people still enjoying breakfast. Marge was starting her clean-up process and paused as she noticed us heading toward her. Marge began the conversation: 'I seem to recall serving this group of boys earlier this morning, so you must be coming back for seconds. How about some of my famous dinosaur pancakes?' Before the boys could take Marge up on her offer, I intervened. I had been gently nurturing a friendly relationship with Marge the previous four mornings, and I was excited about what I planned to do next.

"I began with, 'First of all, Marge, our favorite part of staying at this wonderful campground was enjoying your pancakes each morning. It wasn't just that the pancakes were awesome; it was the love and passion you created and served them with each day. You made the beginning of each day special for us and we wanted to let you know how much that meant to us.' Marge gently interrupted with, 'Those are very kind words. Thank you. I recognize you. You have very well-behaved boys. Isn't your wife that tall, beautiful, blonde woman?' I thanked her for the compliments, admitted I was the lucky man married to my wife, and handed her a thank-you card with a fifty-dollar bill in it. I had written a note to her from our family describing the love, kindness, respect, and care that she exhibited to *each person* that came through her line each day and *what a difference it made in the world.*

"I mentioned that the way she began the day for everyone allowed us to go out and spread that sunshine to others throughout the day. I hadn't planned on it, but she opened the card, read the note, and then attempted to hand the fifty dollars back to me, saying it wasn't necessary. I finally explained to her what it would have cost if we had gone to a restaurant each day, how much we saved by eating her pancakes, and that I was attempting to teach our boys a lesson. She thanked me with the humblest of looks and put the money and the card in her pocket.

"The boys and I had taken about four steps away when I heard Marge say, 'Hey!' I paused, turned around, and looked at her eyes, which now had tears in them. 'Where are you from?' she asked. 'Michigan,' I replied. Now normally this would not be the end of the interchange of conversation. You would anticipate that someone would say something like, 'Oh, that's nice,' or, 'What part of Michigan?' or, 'I've been to Michigan,' or, 'I have relatives that live there.' But it *wasn't meant to be* with Marge. As I paused for a response, Marge just smiled and went back to the task of cleaning up.

"The boys and I headed back to the motor home, ready for the next adventure that would begin that day. The conversation between Marge and I had ended. Or had it? I couldn't help but wonder how the relationship I had enjoyed with Marge for less than an hour each day over the five days would impact the conversation she may have with the next person wearing a shirt or hat indicating they were from Michigan. Would that person automatically be held in high regard, based solely on the brief relationship that finished as a friendship between Marge and our family? Personally, I wanted to believe that the relationship skills I had developed represented *everyone* living in Michigan extremely well. I wanted to believe that what our sons observed that day would solidly add to their foundation of life and serve them well throughout their future in regards to relationships. What do you believe?

"My time with you today has come to an end. I came here to share with you what I have learned about the power of relationships and how it can be the most important tool in your 'personal toolbox for life' that you can possess. So I present to you **The Gift of Relationships.** Remember, this particular tool, and the impact it can have, is designed not only for your career life but for every single aspect of life you will experience. I've shared with you what it is and why it's so important to each of your lives. Utilize the tool called 'The Gift of Relationships' for the betterment of not just yourself but the world. And remember, everything you think, everything you say, all of your actions … they all add up to your character. Character drives trust. Trust drives relationships."

THE GIFT OF TELLING THE TRUTH AND OWNING A MISTAKE

James was in trouble. He knew he was in trouble; he just didn't know what to do about it. Today was Saturday, and just the night before he had blown it. He made a choice he *knew* was wrong. He knew it was wrong beforehand. He knew it was wrong as he did it. He knew it was wrong immediately after he had done it. Why, oh why, had he made such a bonehead decision and put so much at risk? All he could think of was all of the people who would be disappointed in him, all of the people who had believed in him, and all of the people who would suffer as a result of his decision.

James needed help, and he needed it yesterday. The terrible consequences of his decisions were just germinating, and he wanted to stop the growth. He knew that doing nothing and hoping the situation would just go away wasn't going to help. He had woken up at 7:00 a.m. with a nauseous feeling and his head throbbing. Still, he wanted to see if he could make things right without having to suffer the painful consequences of what he had done. If only he could control the video of him chugging beer and prevent it from hitting social media, then he might have a chance. That is, until someone sent him a copy with a "dying laughing" emoji attached. And to think it was one of his best friends who had shot the video, unbeknownst to him, and had texted it to him. To top it off, his parents were still up when he got home over two hours after his curfew. They were furious. Things were bad.

Through chatter at his high school he had heard about this strange building called the Answer Discovery, and he decided, based on what he had heard, that it might contain his last opportunity to get out of this mess he had gotten himself into. By 7:50 that morning he was exiting the Answer Discovery and on his way to controlling the damage he had done last night. He just didn't know exactly what controlling the damage would look like. James was so worried about the situation he had not had time to analyze how unique it was when he was inside. All he knew is that he had been told to go to Currie Bennett Park and look for an elderly man sitting on a park bench. His name was Paul, and he would be expecting James.

• • •

James pulled up to the park and got out of his car. He had this feeling of gratitude momentarily come over him as he thought about how fortunate he was that his parents had purchased a car he could utilize during his senior year of high school and whether that was a privilege that would be taken away if his mistake went public. He glanced around and saw a man sitting on a park bench and began heading toward him. As he approached the man, he noticed that the man's face had an incredible look of peace and calm on it. James was about twelve feet away when Paul spoke.

"Wonderful morning, James! I understand you're in a predicament and that you'd like to talk about it. Won't you join me on this bench and begin to share your story?"

James sat down. Before he began to speak, he felt a little awkward trying to communicate with Paul while both of them were facing the same way rather than at a table facing each other. Paul could sense what was happening, so he set out to calm James down a little and explain why he preferred to utilize a park bench for their discussion.

"Before you begin, maybe I should go first and explain why we're sitting on a park bench." Paul continued, "When my boys were in their middle school and high school years, they were in love with basketball. Although we never felt that they would end up in the NBA, both my wife and I succumbed to that peer group pressure called FOMO."

"Are you talking about 'fear of missing out'?" inquired James.

"Correct. When you see everyone else doing something, it's easy to justify embracing the herd mentality and doing the same thing, even when your gut questions whether it's the right thing to do. So we signed our kids up with the first travel team that would accept them and began heading to tournaments each weekend. Looking back, I've come to realize that the return on investment, or ROI, of being on a travel team wasn't as powerful and impactful in their life as we hoped it would be. But there was one takeaway that I came to treasure that I never would have experienced had it not been for our FOMO."

"What was that?" asked James.

Paul answered:

"Well, first I'd like to acknowledge that some of the very best lessons in life occur during situations that we would normally consider to be time invested with no particular value, but they turn out to be an invaluable opportunity to learn. This is where a choice of perspective becomes such a valuable tool. The key takeaway from the travel basketball experience that had the greatest positive impact on my life at that time was what I call 'Windshield Time.' When we first started traveling to tournaments, I wondered how the time spent traveling could best be utilized, so I started to introduce 'deep thought' conversations with our boys. What I came to realize is that they would share information with me that they would not have in a different environment. I wondered why, and as I began to think it through, I realized that both of us were facing the same direction, our eyes looking forward. We had removed body language and facial expressions from the equation of understanding, and yet, because we were both present in the car together, it differed greatly from something like a phone call or a conversation at home. The kids were not only more honest but more willing to share thoughts on sensitive subjects. That never would have occurred if we were sitting at the kitchen table facing each other or in the family room sitting in a way that allowed direct eye contact.

"As soon as I adopted this new perspective on travel teams, I immediately put it to the best use I could, constantly discussing the most valuable lessons I had learned in life and attempting to pass those lessons on and measure how my kids felt about those subjects. It ended up being the perfect opportunity to talk about the tough subjects, like drugs, alcohol, sex, faith, relationships, friendships, and the impact of good and bad choices. Windshield Time turned out to be one of the most valuable parenting tools I've encountered. It's actually the reason that we're sitting on this park bench this morning. It presents an opportunity for me to be nonjudgmental of you and for you to share with me without feeling judged. Wouldn't you agree that it's the most comfortable opportunity for you to share with me why our paths are crossing this morning?"

"I do now that you've explained why," said James. "I should probably start at the beginning. To be honest, I've lived a life of privilege thus far," he continued. "My parents are still married and love each other. I have a sister, three years older, on a path to be a pediatrician, and I have a younger brother who's a freshman at the same school I attend. He has disabilities but is fully included in the regular classroom. I know he looks up to me. My father works hard to provide for us. He owns a small business whose industry has been declining over the last decade, causing him to work extra hard attempting to survive the downturn. My parents wanted my mom to be a stay-at-home mom to help us make good decisions throughout our life, and they were willing to give up certain things the extra money would have allowed us to do to make that happen. We all volunteer for several nonprofits in the community, and I admit it brings all of us lasting joy when we do. My parents scraped enough money together to provide me with an older but well-maintained car so that I could drive my brother and me to school each day and use it for a summer job later this year."

James paused just long enough for Paul to say, "I would have to agree with your earlier statement that you have lived a privileged life thus far."

"That's just the point!" exclaimed James. "I made a mistake last night that totally screwed up my entire life. If a video that was taken of me last night gets out to social media, I will have given up everything that means anything to me. I need advice on how to stop that video from getting spread around before it completely ruins me. Can you help me?"

When Paul replied, "I think I can," James experienced an immediate reduction of stress and anxiety, believing that Paul was about to somehow eliminate the video from existence. "I'll need some additional information. Why don't you tell me exactly what happened."

James couldn't believe that he was about to share the awful truth with someone he had just met, but there was something about this man, along with sitting on the bench looking forward, that allowed him to open up and spill what had happened the previous night. "As I look back, last night I allowed peer group pressure to make a decision for me that I knew was wrong—but I did it anyway. I'm a co-captain of the basketball team at school and the second-leading scorer thus far this season. Last night we won the district championship, which propels us into a regional tournament, receiving the number one seed. Regionals start next Friday night. Some friends from school had a party last night in their basement to celebrate. Their parents were home but are pretty liberal with alcohol, as long as it's consumed in their house and under their supervision. Everyone was chanting for me to chug a beer to celebrate the win … so I did. I didn't realize at the time that someone was videoing me doing that with their phone. It turns out that it was one of the people I used to think of as one of my best friends. Now I'm not so sure, because I don't trust that he won't put it out there on social media. He texted me a copy of it early this morning. Don't you see? If he posts that on social media, it means I'll be immediately kicked off the basketball team. I'll let down my teammates, my coaches, my fellow students, our school, my parents, my brother and sister, our neighbors, the entire community, my chances for a basketball scholarship at college. If that video gets out today, my life as I know it will be basically over." Tears began to flow, even though he was trying hard to control his emotions as he recalled how he had thrown his life away the previous night.

"Over?" Paul mused. "I think not. What if there were a chance for your life to be improved because of all this?"

James jumped in, "I'm not sure I follow. How could my life even remotely improve?" He was beginning to doubt whether coming here was a good decision.

Paul continued, "Hang with me for a minute. Let's say we're able to squash the video and prevent it from ever hitting social media. I wonder what everyone who witnessed you chugging that beer would say about you, knowing what you were potentially putting in jeopardy by doing so, at your twenty-year high school reunion. It would probably be the most influential experience they witnessed that would be used to describe your total character to someone else at the reunion, whether it's an honest reflection or who you really are or not. Is it possible that, because they saw you get away with breaking the rules and suffering zero consequences, they may assume that you probably cheated in high school, in college, and that you were someone who would cheat on their spouse or at work just to get ahead?"

"Whoa, hold on a minute, Paul. You're getting a little deep here. Am I missing something?"

Paul smiled compassionately. "Wouldn't you agree that if this video got out on social media today, and your worst fears came true, that your classmates would think of you the exact same way at your twenty-year reunion as they would if you got away with it?"

"Maybe...but what's your point?" James said as he was beginning to break down.

Paul gently pushed. "Who has total control over what people will say about you at any point in the future?"

"The person who has control over the video right now," James said, feeling his anxiety beginning to increase again.

"The fact is that each of us has total control over what others think of us and our character. In our house we have a plaque that says, THOUGHTS BECOME WORDS, WORDS BECOME ACTIONS, ACTIONS BECOME CHARACTER, CHARACTER IS EVERYTHING. All you did last night was put a little dent in your character. That dent has the possibility of serving you well for the remainder of your life here on earth. It can be a reminder that we all make mistakes, that it's how we respond to the mistake that defines our true character rather than the mistake itself. Don't you also have control over the video right now, being that your so-called friend sent it to you in the form of a text?" Paul inquired.

"Yes," James responded. "I sent him back a text asking him to delete it from his phone, but he hasn't responded yet."

Paul knew the time was right to throw out an absurd question. "What would you say if there were a way to eliminate the worry of your friend posting the video of you chugging a beer on social media?"

"Are you joking? That's exactly why I came here. How do I do that?"

Paul hesitated for just a second and said, "You post it first."

James wasn't sure he'd heard right, so he asked him to repeat it. "*WHAT?!?*"

"Our discussion needs to go deeper, James. Right now you are totally focused on what people are going to think of you right now, yet what's more important is what people will think of you in the future. It's more important for you to consider what a potential college basketball coach, who has control over scholarships for his team, thinks of you as they recruit. It's more important what a potential employer thinks of you when you look for a job. It's more important what a potential future spouse thinks of you when they're considering spending the rest of their life with you that really counts. All you did last night was succumb to the peer group pressure that led you to making a bad choice. That choice is now in the past and can't be changed. But what you do today about that bad choice may influence the rest of your life. Are you willing to take action now in an attempt for this whole incident to have a positive influence on the rest of your life, or just allow things to play out believing that there isn't *any* result you'd be willing to live with for the rest of your life?"

James attempted to process all that Paul was throwing at him. He was feeling a little overwhelmed. "Wow … I'm still trying to wrap my mind around the idea that I should post it before anyone else does. I'm not sure I could even comprehend how that would be the right thing to do."

Paul responded,

"I anticipated that you would be hesitant, and I want to explain it in a way that will paint a mental picture of how this whole incident could work in your favor and improve your life moving forward. Let's say that you and I discuss and identify all of the people who will be disappointed by what you did last night. Then we create a video with you apologizing to the different groups we identify. You tell them that you made a mistake, that you're holding yourself accountable, that you accept all of the consequences of your poor choice, including being removed from the basketball team.

"Next you communicate that the only positive thing that can occur moving forward is your hope that coming clean and telling the truth about what you did, and people hearing it from you first, will prevent others from making a similar mistake at any point in their life. You can post that video first, before the video with you chugging a beer hits social media. It can be a pivotal, positive, and powerful moment, but you need to post first.

"Further, right after posting your apology, you share your story with the superintendent of your school system and ask him if he'll help you use this mistake you made to prevent other students from making the same mistake. You then ask him if he would consider standing beside you as you tell your family what you've done and then contact the local media. He would add credibility to the sincerity of your admission and apology. If he accepts your request and is willing to help, you head home and have a discussion, which will be difficult but worthwhile, with your family.

"Then, with your family and the superintendent present, you notify a reporter to admit you made a mistake, you're accepting the consequences of the mistake, and you feel it's best that they hear it from you first. Further, knowing the video of you chugging is going to end up on social media soon after your apology video post no matter what, you share a link to the two videos uploaded to social media. Right after that, you take a few minutes to grieve, preferably with your family, until you're ready to head to the police station. Taking a few moments to grieve, surrounded by people who love you, is an important step in being able to continue forward on a positive path.

"If the media gets it right, they'll realize that the real story isn't about the mistake you made; it's about how you handled it. Handling it this way shows maturity, character, and leadership skills. Those are the areas that college coaches, future employers, and potential future spouses care most about. It's the only path that prevents what happened last night from having a negative impact on the rest of your life and offers what may end up being a positive opportunity that you will benefit from for the rest of your life."

James had been softly crying as Paul laid out this plan. He had experienced a wide range of emotions already today and wasn't sure how much more he could handle. James then shared with Paul what he was experiencing. "Look, I've listened to everything you've told me and both my heart and my head are moving in the direction you're suggesting, but I'm afraid. I don't think I can do this. All I feel right now is fear."

Paul's mind revisited all of the times he had felt the exact same way. It took some trial and error to develop the perspective he was about to share with James. That's why he spoke softly when he said, "James, in situations like this there's a chance that fear just might not go away. You might have to do it afraid." For the first time since James had sat on the bench, he looked over and directly into Paul's eyes. He noticed that Paul's eyes were red and that Paul had been shedding tears as he went through describing to him the power of honesty and trust. That's what this was really all about: honesty and trust. James realized at that moment that the most important part of any relationship was trust and that trust can only be obtained, and maintained, with complete honesty in everything someone says, does, and posts. It dawned on him that telling the truth first provided hope for his short-term and long-term future. Trying to hide from the truth only *created negative anxiety that could be with him the rest of his life.*

Paul was right. James needed to do this even if he had to do it afraid. Paul looked directly at James and said, "James, one of the metaphors that has helped me do things afraid is: The sun will rise tomorrow, just as it did today. I've utilized it like a refresh button on a computer screen. If you think about it, the only thing that's fair in this world is that every human inhabitant is given exactly twenty-four hours each and every day. No one gets less, no one gets more. What we choose to do with that twenty-four hours is completely up to us. Each new day is a gift. Now, this current twenty-four-hour period may be one of the most important in your life. What can you do so that when you wake up tomorrow you'll feel good about what you did today?"

"Honestly, Paul, I think I should identify the people who will be hurt by what I did and create that video with my admission of guilt and sincere apology. Would you be willing to help me? Like right now?"

"It would be my privilege!" proclaimed Paul. "I think we should go over what you want to accomplish with this video, write down the important points, including the why, on this blank four-by-six card I just happen to have with me, and then record it right now, before you have the chance to overanalyze the intent."

James paused for a second, looked at Paul, and then asked, "Why did you add 'including the why' when you were talking about the important points?"

"Great question." Paul went on, "If people are going to believe you're sincere, it's not enough to just apologize. Anyone can say they're sorry. Famous people do it all the time in hopes that they'll be forgiven by the public for what they did. It doesn't mean they're contrite. They're just checking off the task of publicly saying sorry, allowing them to not have to change what got them in trouble in the first place. Sometimes the only thing they are really sorry about is that they got caught. Someone who's genuinely sorry shows they are by making immediate changes in their life, ensuring that what happened never happens again. Then they have to allow time to provide the proof and evidence that they were sincere. Successful sincerity can often be accepted at the time of the apology when someone takes the time to say why they did what they did, why it was wrong, and why they need to correct what happened to the best of their ability. James, are you ready to do that?"

James answered right away, "I believe it's the best path forward from where I am currently at. I think I'm ready. Let's go ahead and write down those important points, go over the why, and finish each point with what I plan to do about it."

"I support you," said Paul, and with that they focused on preparing for what James would say. After twenty minutes they agreed that James was prepared for what he was about to do and that it didn't have to be perfect, just sincere. James gave Paul his cell phone to record with, stood in front of Paul with his note card in his hand, and attempted to control his breathing. His heart was pounding, and he needed to calm himself down as much as possible. Then he gave Paul the "go" sign.

"My name is James Eastman. I attend Lincoln High. Some of you will know me. Many of you watching this won't. I made a life-changing mistake last night, and I need to own it and accept the consequences that my actions will bring. I was videoed chugging a beer, and a copy of it will probably end up on social media later today. That my mistake was caught on video doesn't have anything to do with the fact that I made a horrendous choice and should have known better.

"My parents raised me to resist peer group pressure for things that

I know are wrong… but I succumbed. My teammates have looked up to me for leadership and positive decision-making, and I've let them down. I'm immediately removing myself from the basketball team because of what I did, which I know lets my teammates and coaches, our school, and our entire community down. Since what I did broke the underage drinking laws, I am going to turn myself into the police and accept the consequences of breaking that law.

"Isn't it amazing, all of the negative consequences that are occurring in my life all because of about ten seconds of poor decision-making? I've realized that the only possible good that can come from those ten stupid seconds are two things: First, if witnessing the pain and suffering related to that one poor decision that I'll be enduring for potentially the rest of my life … well … if that can prevent just *one* other person from making a similar mistake, then the pain will have been worth it. The second possible good that can come from my poor choice is that I will never again allow peer pressure to influence me to make a choice I know is wrong. I'll have the rest of my life to consistently provide proof that I've done just that.

"Each new day will provide an opportunity for me to consistently do the right thing in all that I do, say, and post on the internet. A couple of minutes ago I heard that 'the sun will rise tomorrow, just as it did today,' but I guess I didn't realize what that really meant … until just right now. But moving forward in life, I will see that saying as a sign of hope. So … I guess that's about all I have to say.

"As soon as I post this, I'm off to first apologize to my family and ask for their understanding and support as I accept the consequences of my poor choice last night. Then, I plan on visiting the police station and contacting the local media so that they all hear it from me first. I'm hoping my parents will be with me when I do. Next, I'll attempt to meet with my coach and teammates to apologize face to face. Finally, I'll attempt to meet with the school superintendent to see what opportunities may exist that will help me become a positive example to others rather than the negative example I provided last night. To the rest of the school and to our entire community … I am sincerely sorry. I hope you can find it in your hearts to forgive me and consider, someday, giving me a second chance to earn your trust."

James nearly fell as he attempted to sit back down on the bench. Paul, who had been recording the video for James, could see that James was emotionally spent and he knew that there was more for James yet to do this day. He slid over close to James and put his arm around his back with his hand on his shoulder and gently said, "You will never regret the words you just said. There's a great future life for you contained within those words. You see, James, what we did previously determines who we are today, but it's what we do today that will determine who we are tomorrow. Based on what you're doing today, I'd venture that your tomorrows are going to shine brightly. Be patient and be consistent."

Paul gave James his phone, and, with shaking hands, James posted the video they had just recorded. Although he felt spent, James looked at Paul, searching for the words to see if Paul might consider coming with him as he attempted to tell his parents what had happened. Paul glanced at James and said, "Would you mind if I went with you and offer my support as you meet with your parents, the media, and the police? I believe in you, James, and I think it may help." James, attempting to hold back a flood of tears, was speechless as his emotions hit a new level. "By the way, when we met I didn't share my last name with you. It's Greene." James's eyes widened as he connected the dots. Paul softly smiled and added, "Paul Greene, school superintendent. What say we start to head to your home? Might be best if I drive."

Upon arrival at James's house, his parents listened intently as James explained what had happened, with Paul helping James's parents see the potential for positive outcomes. As James finished telling his parents what had happened, what he was doing about it, and what he had learned, the three of them embraced silently as tears flowed freely. His younger brother with disabilities joined the group hug, as proud of James as he had ever been. Paul stood by, grateful that he could experience such a powerful moment between a child, his parents, and his brother. James's parents, in that sweet and tender moment, realized that their boy had just taken a giant leap forward in his quest to become the man they had dreamed he would turn out to be.

By now it was about 10:00 that Saturday morning, and James, his parents, and Paul entered the ranch-style home that James had lived in his entire life. With his parents and school superintendent by his side, James called the number he had looked up on the internet that would connect him to the sports editor of the local newspaper. Sarah Miller had just finished an article that would be published that same day about last night's district basketball game.

"Sports, this is Miller." Sarah's energy was always high when she was writing, especially when she finished right as her deadline expired. "Hello … anybody there?" she continued.

"Y-yes, oh, I'm sorry … Ms. Miller?" James asked.

"That's the name I used answering when you called. How can I help?"

"My name is James Eastman and I—"

James was interrupted by Sarah. "The captain-on-the-basketball-team-that-secured-a-big-win-last-night-in-the-district-finals James Eastman?"

"Correct," James said sheepishly.

"Nice game last night, Eastman. How can I help you?" Sarah sensed that this phone call was about to get interesting.

"Well, I just emailed you two videos," James continued, "and the first shows me making a poor choice chugging a beer last night. The second is an attempt on my part to right a wrong."

It seemed like forever, but finally, after about twelve seconds of silence, Sarah asked James, "Did you just say what I *think* I heard you say?"

James replied, "Yes, I did."

Sarah asked James if she could place him on hold as she opened the email and watched the two videos. James had had his phone on speaker so his parents and Paul could listen to both sides of the conversation. While he was on hold, waiting for Sarah to return to the call, he glanced at the three adults in his presence and was thankful for the warm and thoughtful looks on all of their faces. It provided him encouragement that he was doing the right thing. He would recall this moment later in his life as the beginning of his acceptance that his life could actually be better moving forward *because of* what had happened instead of *in spite of* what had happened. It would turn out to be one of the most critical lessons of his life, which he would eventually share openly with others.

Meanwhile, Sarah had just finished watching both videos. She sat in her chair, closed her eyes, and slowed down her racing mind. After watching James's confession video, she realized that her years of experience gave her the intuition that there may be a bigger story here than what the videos revealed at first blush. She popped back on the line with James. "In your second video, James, you said you were going to the police station to admit you broke the law. Would you be willing to let me be there when you do?"

James shot a quick glance at his parents and Paul and received confirming looks. "That would be fine. I had intended to head over there as soon as I completed this call."

"Great," said Sarah. "I'll meet you there."

As James walked up to the local law enforcement building with his parents and Paul close behind, he took a deep breath, opened the door, and walked inside. They all noticed a woman up at the police counter chatting with an officer, who turned out to be Police Chief Carl Hamilton. James walked up to them, saw the press pass that Sarah was wearing with her name on it, and nervously said to the police officer, "My name is James Eastman. I'm here to report that I broke the law last night, and I'd like to turn myself in."

Carl had been prepped by Sarah regarding what was about to happen and suggested that they all come into the police training room and sit at a round table where James could tell him his story. When James had finished telling his story and showing the two videos to the police chief, Carl began to ask some questions, the first of which was directed to James.

"James, what's your goal in coming here and sharing all of this self-incriminating evidence with me?"

James replied, "After talking with Paul this morning, I came to realize that this poor choice I made last night was going to have an impact on the rest of my life and that I could either utilize my mistake as a crutch or as a springboard. I've realized that my poor choice isn't about the fact that I got caught … it's really about the fact that succumbing to peer group pressure can put any of us in a position where we make a decision that we know is wrong. It's a lesson that I'll carry with me the rest of my life."

Carl turned to the school superintendent, Paul, and asked, "Will James have to be suspended from the team immediately, eliminating the possibility of him playing in the regionals?"

Paul responded, "There is no alternative but to suspend him for the rest of the season, including the playoffs."

Chief Carl then turned to James's parents and asked them what they thought about all of this. James's mother answered, "All in all, our son is a good kid. We've raised him to understand that all of the choices we make have consequences, and depending on the choice, the consequence may be good or the consequence may be bad. We acknowledge that he made a mistake, and we support that he has to face the consequences of that mistake. We have confidence in his future, given his willingness to experience the pain that's resulting from his poor choice. Finally, both my husband and I think this event represents a foundational opportunity that could serve James well for the rest of his life, and we're willing to help him 'anchor this pain' so that he never wants to experience this kind of pain again."

Curious, the chief asked, "What do you mean by 'anchor this pain'?"

James's dad joined in, saying, "When you use an anchor, you keep something in place. Storms can come and go, but a good anchor holds on and holds firm. It's a little metaphor we developed with our children in a deeper discussion of principles. The principles that guide each person's life."

Chief Carl paused. He was beginning to frame this whole situation in his mind, and, frankly, what he was experiencing today was a first. He'd never had a high school student turn himself in for a minor in possession charge, and he had never encountered parents in a situation like this who not only stood by their son but also stood by the law, along with the punishment that law was required to administer. He looked over at Sarah and asked, "What are your thoughts right now on how you're going to report this?"

Sarah had been silent and was taking it all in, absorbing it like a sponge. Her experience as a reporter was allowing her to view the situation from many different perspectives. "James is human, no more so nor less than the rest of us. As humans, we all make mistakes. Mistakes vary and can be grouped according to short-term and long-term impact. Mistakes can further be grouped into categories regarding *level* of impact. Mistakes also vary on *who* is impacted. The reach that mistakes can have on ourselves and others may be narrow, like accidentally hitting your thumb with a hammer when you weren't paying close enough attention to where you were striking, or wide, like the baseball players who allegedly cheated in the 1919 World Series, hurting an entire country and what it stood for. At this point I believe James's mistake could have both short- *and* long-term impact. The level of impact has huge positive potential on what could eventually be millions of people if the handling of his mistake is done with 'maximum positive impact' being the goal. I've never experienced anyone attempting to right a wrong the way James, with the support of his family and the superintendent of schools, is doing today. I have a feel for where I'd like to take this story, but before I do I want to know how the two of you are going to proceed."

Sarah was looking at Chief Carl and Superintendent Paul with piercing eyes, in hopes that they would recognize the power a story with the right perspective could have. She wouldn't have worried about the superintendent had she been present at the park bench meeting James and Paul had earlier, but he hadn't yet indicated what the school's approach was going to be. Chief Carl had a look on his face indicating that he was still processing how to proceed.

Paul took the lead.

"James has agreed that he needs to forfeit his position on the basketball team and serve a three-day suspension from school for what he did. He's a dedicated student scholastically, and the three days shouldn't impact his grades if he attempts to stay current with classwork while he's suspended.

"You're all familiar with Central State University, which is thirty miles west of here. They're a mid-size Division I university. The person who scouts and recruits for the men's basketball team there is a close personal friend of mine. I know if I asked, she'd be willing to attend the regional game this coming Friday, and I could have James sit between us as we cheer for our team. After hearing the story, I believe that she could provide insight into how this whole incident could work to James's advantage in garnering interest from colleges that would be willing to recruit James, with an emphasis on his character traits more than his basketball skills.

"Any credible coach at any level of a sport would agree that character can't be trained, and it's one of the hardest things to correctly identify because everyone is taught to act a specific way when they know someone is watching. Someone told me once that our true character is defined by the things we think, say, and do when we think no one is watching. I've come to believe that's true.

"I also intend to mentor James for as long as he'll allow me to. He's proven to me today that he's willing to listen and take action based on what he's learned from listening. Coaches warmly describe kids like that as 'coachable.' I can help someone like that do great things. So that's the plan I intend to put in place beginning today."

"What about you, Carl? What's the next step?" Sarah had been taking notes, attempting to capture all that Paul was saying…and was it ever hard to capture so many insights. Her mind had to battle the temptation of fleshing those insights out to their fullest potential. She had wanted to stop Paul at several points and ask follow-up questions, but she resisted.

Chief Carl picked up the dialogue.

"Yeah…next step…wow…this is one of those rare cases that they don't teach you about in law enforcement school. Having said that, we are taught to perform quick analysis and response. As you gain years of experience, you rely on what your subconscious has learned and your instincts. I might disagree with Paul about the inability to *train* character, because I believe character can be improved if presented in story form and then consistently practiced until mastered. I never want to give up hope. I fully agree that it's one of the hardest things to correctly identify.

"Just think of an officer making a traffic stop and how they're given only seconds to try to determine the character of the individual they just pulled over. Thankfully, we're given tools and strategies to help us with that assessment. Which brings me back to James. What he did is classified differently than a true crime, and the punishment is typically that the minor is given a ticket. In the next fifteen minutes I'm going to have him experience what it would feel like if he was being booked for an actual crime, but it's only for show, and it won't be recorded in any way associated with his name.

"Just going through the booking process is painful, and I'm doing it to James in hopes that the experience will act as a future deterrent. I have the ability to recommend forty hours of community service to be completed within six months for what he did. If he completes the community service and stays true to character, in six months his record will be expunged, eliminating any permanent negative impact for his future career and life.

"I also would like to be a mentor to James if he'll accept my help. I'd appreciate the opportunity to share the lessons I've learned from mistakes I've made myself and the poor choices—and good choices—I've witnessed others making and how those choices worked out for them. I firmly believe that James offers both Paul and me an incredible opportunity to have a positive impact on other teenagers and help prevent them from making poor choices that can have a huge negative impact on the rest of their lives. So many live in the moment, with no care about how that moment will impact their future. James has learned that lesson over the last twenty-four hours."

Sarah was on fire. As she was furiously scribbling her notes, attempting to follow every single word being spoken, she was acutely aware that something special—*really* special—was coming together and beginning to take shape. Every few seconds she'd glance up at James and his parents and attempt to record in her mind's eye the expressions and reactions they exhibited as both Superintendent Paul and Chief Carl presented their plan for moving forward.

"I guess that brings us back to you, Sarah. What are you going to report?" asked Paul. Sarah finished her notes and slowly looked at Carl, Paul, James's parents, and finally at James. She paused and looked deep into James's eyes. She smiled, realizing that there was another story contained within those eyes and that face she was look-ing at—a story so deep she could make it into a novel.

The novel would have to wait for another day. Sarah threw back the question Paul had just asked. "What am I going to report? Let's just say that this story is providing me with material worthy of a Nobel Prize in literature. It's a story that can change and save lives if I pres-ent it and utilize what the story is really about. You've all given me a great gift today—one I wasn't sure I'd ever be given in my career. Thank you! All of you! I promise you won't be disappointed."

With that, Sarah collected her notes and was off. Part of James's future went with her. At that precise moment, after all he had been through the previous twenty-four hours, James felt an overwhelm-ing sense of peace. He pulled a deep breath in through his nose and exhaled through his mouth. He looked at his parents and smiled. Their faces seemed to show concern and sadness but also hope and humble pride. For a fleeting moment James wondered if he would have an opportunity to look at his children that way some day. He moved his eyes to Paul, who had been right there beside him since early this morning.

James seemed to sense that the look on Paul's face was strangely similar to his parents. Then he realized something very profound: Parental love doesn't have to be limited to one's own children. He had an instant desire to learn how he could share that love with oth-ers. The way James felt at that very moment was vastly different than the way he had felt when he woke up earlier that day. It had been such an incredible experience. He wanted to be sure to record in his mind everything that had transpired, in hopes that he could utilize the experience of today to help others in the future. With that, he glanced at Chief Carl, smiled, and said, "Chief, I'm ready for the pain of being booked now. I look forward to the good that will come from the pain of a lesson learned."

Paul wanted the last word before James was booked. Looking deep into James's eyes, he said, "James, you've been given a great gift today: **The Gift of Telling the Truth and Owning a Mistake**. If used wisely, this gift will propel you forward toward an incredible destiny, including roles that will allow you to lead others toward a positive future. Thank you for allowing me to help and support you today. It's meant the world to me." With that, the police chief led James to what would turn out to be a life tool that James would use wisely.

THE GIFT AND POWER
OF FORGIVENESS

Boy, oh boy, was Jennifer mad! Not regular mad, but the worst kind of mad. The kind of mad that had been built upon a foundation of bitterness and anger. She seemed to be actually enjoying and embracing the feeling as, for the third time in the last two minutes, she proved to the world that she had mastered the intricate talent of proper horn usage on her European SUV. Knowing the idiots on the receiving end of her horn-blowing couldn't hear a word she was saying, she spoke her mind while demonstrating her ability to multitask by utilizing her middle finger.

Jennifer seemed to be the only person on this earth who didn't realize how destructive her actions had become. She cussed proficiently as she finally pulled into the parking space in front of the Answer Discovery, perturbed that it had taken more than fifteen minutes to get to the building from her home in this stupid town she lived in. It seemed like every single traffic light turned red just before she got there. As she opened her door to exit her vehicle, she muttered, "Let's get this over with," and proceeded up to the door.

Jennifer entered the Answer Discovery the same way she entered every building (and room for that matter): with a commando-type entrance that indicated that whoever *had* been in charge—well, that person would now be answering to her. "Hello, how about a little help here? HELLO!!!" Jennifer shouted as her eyes scanned the room. But before she heard a response or saw someone, she paused and unknowingly allowed conflict to enter her mind. *Wait a second*, she thought. *The inside of this building doesn't follow the shape nor design of the outside. How can that be?* This thought had totally interrupted her initial strategy, and as she was attempting to quickly adapt to the strangeness of the interior, she jumped about two feet in the air when words suddenly appeared in her mind.

WELCOME, JENNIFER. IT'S GOOD OF YOU TO VISIT TODAY.

While her initial thought was to shout out "Who said that?" she hesitated, lost the sense of urgency to find out, and experienced a feeling of calm that she hadn't experienced in years.

HOW IS IT YOU'D LIKE TO BE SERVED TODAY? entered her brain. Now, normally she would either be freaking out, chalking this up to some magic trick, or figuring that it was some new sort of technology that she just hadn't heard about before. But still, none of those would explain what had happened. She tried to recover her composure and asked, "Isn't this the place that gives answers to people?"

IT'S A PLACE THAT GIVES DIRECTION TO AN ANSWER FOR THOSE THAT OPEN THEIR HEARTS AND MINDS WITH WILLINGNESS TO HEAR AN ANSWER THAT THEY WILL ACCEPT, EMBRACE, AND TAKE ACTION ON.

At this point Jennifer began to slip into her "must have control" thought strategy and blurted out, "Who are you? No wait, I know it's a who even though I can't quite determine your gender. How about *where* are you and why don't you come out so we can talk face to face?"

Her mind received an answer that began, IF THERE WERE TO BE A PERSON STANDING IN FRONT OF YOU, YOUR MIND WOULD IMMEDI-ATELY BE DISTRACTED BY MAKING JUDGMENTS BASED ON WHAT YOU

WERE SEEING. YOU WOULD THEN ATTEMPT TO FORMULATE A STRAT-
EGY TO GAIN CONTROL OF THE SITUATION AND UTILIZE THAT CON-
TROL TO GET YOU YOUR PREDETERMINED ANSWER TO THE REASON
YOU CAME HERE IN THE FIRST PLACE. THAT WOULD HAVE DEFEATED
YOUR INNER THOUGHTS QUESTIONING WHETHER YOU MAY BE WRONG
ABOUT SOME THINGS.

"You—whoever you might be—make it sound like I'm a person
who's broken and needs fixing."

I AM SUGGESTING THAT IF A PERSON IS CONSISTENTLY FRUSTRATED
WITH AND UNHAPPY ABOUT THE WORLD AROUND THEM AND REFUSES
TO ADMIT THAT SOME PART OF THEIR THINKING PROCESS MAY BE BRO-
KEN, THEN THEY ELIMINATE THE OPPORTUNITY TO LIVING A FULFILL-
ING AND JOY-FILLED LIFE THAT GROWS EACH DAY ON A REGULAR BASIS.

Jennifer's mind was swirling with what she had just been presented.
Was she broken? She had been raised to never accept defeat, no matter the consequences. Yet that thought process had led her to driving
here today and entering the building she now stood in. Maybe the
real question wasn't whether she was broken or not. Maybe the real
question was *how* broken, and was there any chance she could overcome her brokenness and experience that joy, growth, and fulfillment
that had just been mentioned? Tears began to form in her eyes. She
hated that. It was a sign of weakness that she had overcome early in
life, believing that it gave people a chance to take advantage of her.
She hadn't succumbed to letting them flow since her early teens, but
right then she felt so weak. Was she broken? It was soft, almost a
whimper, but the words that she had sworn so long ago never to use
came forth from her lips: "Can you help me?"

Jennifer's plea was met with a warm and loving response. COUR-
AGE. TRUST. VULNERABILITY. TRUTH. OPEN-MINDEDNESS. YOU JUST
SUCCESSFULLY CLIMBED OVER THE BIGGEST HURDLE YOU WILL FACE
BY UTILIZING THOSE TRAITS AND DECISIONS AT THE APPROPRIATE

TIME. CAN YOU BE HELPED? YES! WHEN YOU FINALLY ADMITTED TO YOURSELF THAT PARTS OF YOUR LIFE WERE BROKEN, YOU OPENED UP A WHOLE NEW LIFE FOR YOURSELF. NOW YOU CAN BEGIN A PATH TO THE FULFILLING, GROWTH-ORIENTED, AND JOY-FILLED LIFE THAT YOU DESIRE IN YOUR INNERMOST THOUGHTS. THOUGHTS THAT, UP UNTIL TODAY, YOU ONLY SHARED WITH YOURSELF WHEN YOU WERE SURE NO ONE OTHER THAN YOU WAS LISTENING. PLEASE GET IN YOUR VEHICLE AND DRIVE TO 3223 RIVERVIEW ROAD. IT'S A DEAD-END ROAD THAT TRAVELS ALONGSIDE THE AU SABLE RIVER. THERE ARE TEN GLASS PODS RIGHT BESIDE THE RIVER, ABOUT A HUNDRED YARDS FROM EACH OTHER WITH DENSE VEGETATION IN BETWEEN. THEY'RE NUMBERED AND HAVE SMALL AREAS TO PARK NEXT TO THEM. YOU WILL STOP, PARK, AND ENTER POD SEVEN, WHERE YOU WILL MEET AN INDIVIDUAL NAMED RUNNING BEAR. SHE WILL HELP YOU GET TO WHERE YOU WANT TO BE. THANK YOU FOR ASKING FOR HELP. IT'S ONE OF THE MOST POWERFUL GIFTS WE ALL POSSESS BUT STRUGGLE TO USE."

With that the lighting changed ever so slightly, and Jennifer sensed it as a cue to exit the building, enter her vehicle, and begin a new direction to Riverview Road.

* * *

On the way to her new destination, Jennifer found herself driving near the speed limit and was aware that she was not letting everything happening around her have any impact. She wasn't in a hurry and began to ponder why. Yesterday she would have been strategizing how to wrestle control of the situation she was headed toward from the very moment she entered the pod. But today she seemed to have jumped a hurdle that she had placed before herself early in her life. It was exciting... and a little scary. She wasn't ready to share any of these feelings with anyone—especially anyone who knew her—but she knew she was tired. Tired of being frustrated all the time. Tired of being a fault-finding expert. Tired of righteousness regarding *every single issue*. Tired of always being right and spending every single moment of each day attempting to convince others that she was right. She was, wasn't she? Always right? She had built her career and financial success on crushing others, proving them wrong, and publicly exposing their weaknesses and faults, all the while guarding and protecting her own. When it came to the difference between right and wrong, she had always been on the side of right. Hadn't she? Honestly, she could not remember the last time she had thought about the difference between the two. She had always just felt that she was always right and that anyone who didn't agree with her was wrong. She thought about how weak and pathetic she would be if she ever admitted that she may have been wrong about anything.

At that precise instant Jennifer had a moment of doubt. What was she doing? Why didn't she just turn around? Then she reminded herself that she had gone to the Answer Discovery because she was tired of running on the never-ending spinning wheel of life going nowhere. She continued to drive and shortly thereafter turned onto Riverview Road.

All of sudden Jennifer became aware of the natural beauty on either side of the road as it twisted and turned over hills and under tunnels that the trees naturally created. She lamented that she couldn't remember the last time she had paused to embrace and admire nature and all that it offered. She came upon the first pod just as the Au Sable River came into view. The river was about fifty feet wide and, because of the complete clarity of the water, looked to be anywhere from two to four feet deep at any given spot. The sun was shining, and it glimmered off the undulating surfaces created by the gentle flow. The road went back into the forest for about a hundred yards, then swung back toward the river as Jennifer noticed the second pod.

Her mind was racing so much that she hadn't really looked closely at the first pod, but as she slowed to look at the second, she determined that it resembled a tall igloo, maybe twenty-five feet in diameter and approximately fifteen feet tall in the center. She noticed an igloo-type entrance tall enough to walk through, with a clear glass door facing opposite the river view toward the road. In fact, the igloo type structure itself looked to be constructed of frosted glass.

Jennifer had never seen anything like this before. She was about to ponder what a strange and mysterious day this had been so far when she slammed on the brakes just in time to avoid hitting a fawn that was crossing the road after having quenched its thirst in the river. While the fawn continued to casually walk toward its mother, Jennifer felt her heart pounding in her chest. Normally the words "Get a (insert not nice word) grip!" would have been shouted as part of her self-talk when she was alone, but she realized that she really didn't like the way she felt when she talked to herself that way and now pondered how others felt when she addressed them in similar fashion. She had never cared before and couldn't tolerate weak individuals and their whininess. This day just continued to get stranger with every passing minute.

Jennifer began moving forward again down Riverview Road and wondered why it was called a road. Even though it was paved, it seemed like more of a trail from the way it meandered. She continued to meander past other pods, all similar-looking, until she came upon number seven. The parking area was empty, but she noticed the door was propped open. She pulled into the space that appeared to be for vehicles, put her SUV in park, turned off the engine, and just sat in her vehicle. It wasn't that she wasn't in a hurry. She just wanted to savor the moment—a moment of great uncertainty, unlike anything she was accustomed to. She was always in control of everything, until today. She worked on her breathing and lowered her heart rate by a few beats per minute in an attempt to compose herself and enter the pod thingy she was parked next to with confidence to meet with some burly and gruff-sounding woman nicknamed Running Bear.

As Jennifer opened the door and exited her vehicle, something caught her peripheral vision, and as she turned her head she witnessed the last twenty feet of flight right before a bald eagle extended its talons into the water, plucked a brown trout from under the surface, and flew off downriver with its prey secured for a feast. It took her breath away. She had just witnessed a combination of beauty and tragedy occurring in the passage of just a few seconds. There were so many stories that could be told from the eagle's perspective, from the trout's perspective, and from her own as a witness to what had just occurred. And so she stood very still and thought—that is, until she jumped about a foot off the ground as a woman's voice loudly exclaimed, "HÁU!"

"Hey," Jennifer responded. "You may want to gently announce your presence before you make a person's heart skip a beat and—" Jennifer paused. As she had begun speaking, she had turned her head in the direction of the word *háu* and set her eyes upon a beautiful, professionally dressed woman, mid-twenties, with long straight black hair, who was holding her left hand up in the air near the door to pod seven. The woman by the door repeated the word *háu* with a totally blank expression on her face. Jennifer muttered her next words with a little confusion. "I'm sorry, I'm supposed to meet a woman named Running Bear at building seven. Am I in the right place?"

"You are, but I was at least hoping for chuckle, if not a full out laugh, when I greeted you with my pattern interrupter 'háu.' I guess I need to keep working on my delivery. Oh, and no offense taken. Expecting a manly woman is a common occurrence with a name like Running Bear. My birth name is actually Running Bearing Positive, but everyone calls me Running Bear because it's easier to say. In fact, people that know me well prefer to say RB, which works really well."

At this point Jennifer was completely discombobulated. "I'm a little confused . . . so *you* are Running Bear, and did I just hear you correctly when I thought I heard you use the term *pattern interrupter?*" she stammered.

"Well, you get an A for being attentive. Welcome to pod seven. Come on in. There are a couple of stress-free chairs, some fresh iced and filtered water, and an incredible view that will allow us to have a positive conversation about life."

As Jennifer entered the pod, she observed that the curved top was darkened to protect them from the rays of sun but that you were still able to see clearly what was above it. Then she looked out at the curved sides of the pod, acknowledging that it appeared as if there were no glass at all, even though she knew there was. It was the clearest glass she had ever witnessed, and no matter which direction you looked in, it made you feel like you were immersed right in the middle of the beautiful scene of nature. She sensed a feeling of peace and contentment that hadn't been present in her life for decades. And then she snapped back into reality. "I'm not sure why I'm here nor what purpose this will serve. Would you mind explaining why I had to drive to who knows where and meet with someone I know nothing about?"

"Glad to," offered Running Bear, "but did you ever play a game called hopscotch when you were growing up?"

Caught off-guard yet again, Jennifer responded curtly, "Of course, didn't everyone?"

"As I was preparing to meet with you today, I realized that I would need to utilize 'pattern interrupters' throughout our time together in order to address your strong will and desire to always be in control of every situation you find yourself in. It's the only way your mind will be open enough to consider the opportunity to begin a path to a fulfilling, growth-oriented, and joy-filled life that you desire in your innermost thoughts. I will continually interrupt your pattern of attempting to take control of the situation, which is what got you to where you find yourself today. Then I will explain *why* your pattern is inappropriate if you truly want to achieve the life you dream of. I'll then offer an appropriate replacement for the pattern you're so accustomed to, and then, utilizing leverage, anchor the new pattern in place to prevent the old one from attempting to return. If I notice that the direction you're heading in is attempting to re-enlist your control of the situation, I'll interject a pattern interrupter to get you back on track in the direction to solution. The reason you are in this pod with me is because five years ago, for lack of a better way to say it, I was in the same place you find yourself in today. I was a control freak, right about everything, with total disdain for anyone who didn't accept my perspective as I presented it. I didn't care that I wasn't necessarily a nice person; I was juiced each day by righteousness. It was my duty to point it out to people and let them know that they should think like me."

Jennifer interrupted, "Well, that's exactly right. Just like me. I mean, I always know I'm right, and I get so frustrated when people won't acknowledge it."

Running Bear paused for a moment, then realized she had Jennifer's complete attention and didn't need to use another pattern interrupter just yet.

"Every day I craved that juice that came from always being right, until one day I recalled reading an article a few months earlier debating righteousness versus happiness. It said you couldn't be both righteous and happy. My righteous mind immediately attempted to disprove that theory, but all of my attempts failed. What I realized was that I *thought* that being righteous made me happy, you know … kind of like people who appear happiest when they have lots to complain about … but, truth be told, what I experienced most by being righteous was *anger*.

"I realized I had perfected the art of being angry all the time. Righteousness was the perfect fuel for anger. I knew I believed that anger was one of the most powerful emotions we humans possess and that it fell into two categories: destructive anger and motivational anger. What I couldn't see or admit was that I had fooled myself into believing that my daily use of righteousness was fueling my motivational anger when it was really high-octane fuel for destructive anger.

"It was that article that compared righteousness to happiness that began to open my eyes to the fact that I was missing out on happiness. But at the time, it didn't impel me to take any action to change. Today I would substitute the word *love* for the word *happiness*. I wasn't giving, nor receiving, love … at all … ever … with anyone. Oh, at times I thought I was experiencing love. Like when I was in a relationship for two years. I had anticipated that, on our second anniversary of dating, he would pop the question at this nice restaurant we were at. When the question didn't come, I blew up.

"I was so pumped up with righteousness that I told him that if he didn't ask me to marry him right then, we were just wasting each other's time. He stared at me with big, sad eyes for thirty seconds. I stood up, called him a loser, drove home enraged, walked into my home, fell on the living room floor, and cried harder than I had ever cried before. I had never felt so alone at any other time in my life. That night, I began the most destructive behavior I could think of: cutting."

"You mean cutting your skin with a knife?" Jennifer blurted out.

"It was actually a razor blade that I preferred. There were times I cut so deep I'd have to later super-glue the cut back together. I have the scars that constantly remind me of the mental state I used to allow myself to slip into. My anger would boil over, and cutting seemed the only thing that would turn the heat down to a simmer."

By now Jennifer's eyes were as big as saucers. "So then what happened?"

"I was spent. I realized that I hadn't won. Righteousness had won, which means that I had lost. I had never seen myself losing at anything before. And then it got worse. I became obsessed with the injustice that my people had been dealing with for over three hundred years as their land and their lives were stripped away. I saw it as slavery that wasn't impacted by, nor included with, the Emancipation Proclamation. One could build a case for Native Americans still not being *free*.

"It was at this point that I developed a righteousness that had bypassed the motive of attempting to make a difference for all Native Americans and flowed into one of the most self-destructive paths a human could take. I drove to a national park near where I lived, went to the edge of a cliff, and contemplated removing all of the pain from my life by ending it. I sat near the edge, took some deep calming breaths, and willed myself to pause, consider, and determine if this was the path that offered the very best solution for my life.

"This moment—this brief pause before I made a final decision on whether I wanted to live or not—allowed me to assess the patterns and habits that had led me to this unbearable place. I wasn't where I wanted to be and, to be honest, I realized I had never developed an image in my mind as to what I wanted my life to be defined by. I subconsciously knew I didn't really want to end my life, and cutting wasn't cutting it as a temporary solution to mask the pain anymore. What I wanted was a path forward that I could embrace, defined by getting to where I wanted to go, even though I couldn't clearly define that place.

"As I was reflecting on my life, I realized that what I really wanted was the experience of a path to a fulfilling, growth-oriented, and joy-filled life . . . just like you indicated earlier today. One that wasn't filled with so much destructive anger. I realized that I had been fooling myself with labeling destructive anger as righteousness. Like I just indicated, growing up as a Native American, it's nearly inevitable that you will base your life and personality on righteousness if you choose to focus on all that's been taken away from you and your tribe rather than having gratitude for all that you have been given.

"For much of my life, I chose righteousness. The key word in that last sentence is 'chose.' I had never thought of my life as a choice that I was able to make every single morning that I awoke. Then, while recalling the article I had read about righteousness, I had an epiphany, realizing that I wanted to experience joy each day rather than anger. I realized that giving and receiving joy every day of my life was what I craved. I wanted to be loved. This desire grew in my heart and in my mind for about an hour, and I realized that it was maybe the most important moment in my life."

At this point, Jennifer was dumbfounded by all she was hearing. This was exactly what she had been going through this very day. She managed to get three words out of her lips, saying, "What happened next?"

RB noticed she hadn't needed to employ a pattern interrupter and was thankful she had Jennifer's full attention ... at least for the moment. She had been carefully crafting her words and wanted to create in Jennifer both a desire and, more importantly, a commitment to change from the path she had been following and embrace the path Running Bear was about to supplant with a firm anchor to hold the new path in place.

"What happened next is fascinating. At that very moment I made the distinction between destructive anger and motivational anger and realized that I had been fueling my destructive anger under the mask of righteousness. I knew myself well enough to know that if I didn't take action right then, at that very moment, I would allow righteousness to slip right back into my mind and justify the life that I now understood was making me miserable. There are moments in all of our lives that are pivotal, and most times we don't see them as such until long after we've experienced the results of that moment. But not this time. So, I jumped."

"What do you mean? You jumped … off the *cliff*?" Jennifer had moved to the edge of her seat.

"I jumped *up*. Then, following the trail back to where I had parked, I jumped into my car and headed home. Once I arrived home I searched for that article about righteousness versus happiness. It took me a half hour to find it, but I did. I reread the article about comparing these two polar opposite emotions with a new perspective. Suddenly I glanced over at the clock and noticed that it was 11:33 at night.

"At that very moment, I made the distinction between destructive anger and motivational anger and admitted what I had thought about on the cliff earlier, which is that I had been fueling my destructive anger under the mask of righteousness. I just hadn't wanted to admit it the last time I read the article. I knew anger was powerful and finally realized that it could be just as useful for good as it had been in my life for evil.

"I knew myself well enough to know that if I didn't take action right then, at that very moment, I would allow righteousness to slip right back into my mind and justify the life that I now understood was making me miserable. There are moments in all of our lives that are pivotal, and most times we don't see them as such until long after we've experienced the results of that moment.

"I jumped back in my car and drove directly to the Answer Discovery, negotiating with God what I would be willing to do if only the place was still open. I wasn't sure that I could maintain my commitment to action if I had to wait until the following day. I arrived and went up to the door. It opened and interrupted my normal pattern of attempting to take control. It's almost like it had known all along that I was coming and when I would arrive. As I entered, I felt this tremendous weight lift from my shoulders and had a real sense of peace surge through my body."

Nearly shouting, Jennifer exclaimed, "That's the same feeling I experienced earlier today! I'm not sure I'd be here right now if I hadn't."

"I know," RB continued, "and it's difficult to describe, but it was exactly what I needed. First, I had to be willing to accept the unique way I was being communicated to once inside the building. It was different than anything I had ever experienced before. Then, I was asked to describe what I was seeking, and I said that I was tired. Tired of living each day mad at the world, mad at circumstances, and mad at individuals who didn't see things the way I saw them. I said I was ready to walk down a path toward a fulfilling, growth-oriented, and joy-filled life but didn't know how to get there. Suddenly, I was told to get in my vehicle and drive to 3223 Riverview Road. It would be a dead-end road that travels alongside the Au Sable River. There would be ten glass pods right beside the river, about a hundred yards from each other with dense vegetation in between. They'd be numbered and have small areas to park next to them. I was told to stop, park, and enter pod three, where I would meet Heather Holly. By then it was after midnight, and I had to resist the time concern and stay committed to where the motivational anger was leading me. Plus, there was a full moon in a cloudless sky, boldly attempting to mimic the sun, and I had been told to go to pod three. Three is my favorite number."

Jennifer interrupted again. "This is so weird. Seven is *my* favorite number."

Running Bear continued,

"Looking back, I laugh because Heather greeted me as I was exiting my car, on this incredible moonlit night, and threw out a pattern interrupter to me, asking, 'There isn't any chance you're afraid of snakes, are you?' Well, you can imagine where my mind went to, and I immediately shot back at her, 'Why do you ask?' to which she casually replied, 'Oh, no real reason, I was just curious. Welcome. I'm so glad you're here on this wonderful and beautiful night. Come on into pod three and let's sit a spell.'

"As I walked toward the pod entrance, I kept noticing a unique and distinct sound that was coming from the water. I didn't realize it at the time, but it turned out to be a natural pattern interrupter. I asked Heather what the sound was, and she told me that there was an insect hatch occurring and that the trout inhabiting the river were in a feeding frenzy, catching the insects on the surface of the river before they had a chance to lift off into the air. Although my attention had been diverted as I entered the pod, my mind quickly went back to the reason I was there in the middle of the night and how I desperately wanted to find an answer. I'm about to share with you what Heather shared with me.

"Heather told me that my righteousness was a self-defense mechanism that I triggered in an attempt to gain control. I craved that control to eliminate being vulnerable . . . to anyone . . . at any time. Heather further told me that while I pursued control in every situation through the use of righteousness, the end result was isolation masked as control. Isolation removed the possibility of the three things all humans crave on a daily basis: appreciation, respect, and love.

"Righteousness hadn't allowed me to be open to any of those, and so my savings accounts for those three were empty, while my righteousness account overflowed with value that wasn't accepted anywhere. Since I never wanted to be vulnerable and open-hearted and risk being hurt, I had closed off any opportunity that came my way to be appreciated, respected, and loved. My good tank was empty, and my evil tank never appeared less than full."

Running Bear paused as a tear ran down her cheek, causing Jennifer's eyes to form tears as she said to RB, "I'm so sorry . . . this is just so sad."

"You mistake my tears as those of sadness rather than the tears of joy created by the powerful emotion of finally realizing how broken I was and that a strategy appeared to be unwrapping itself in front of me that would allow me to turn my life around."

Jennifer's mind was whirling as she was experiencing visions of her own daily life in the words that Heather had spoken to Running Bear several years ago. Jennifer wondered if her own tears were coming forth because of her empathy for RB, or if she was realizing that the person being described as Running Bear years ago was the mirror image of who she was today.

Running Bear continued. "Heather told me that if I wanted to change—*really* wanted to change—I would need to see and accept that my current routines, life strategies, immediate reactions to situations, and management of my relationships were broken, *why* they were broken, what they needed to be replaced with, *why* they were being replaced with new choices, and what the end result would be from the moment I took action with these changes for the remainder of my life."

"Wow, that's a lot to ask," Jennifer interjected.

"That's what I immediately thought as I witnessed myself falling back into my failed thought process. I protested and accused Heather of being harsh and judgmental. Then Heather looked me right in the eye and said, 'Don't move; there are two bear cubs approaching our pod with their mother right behind.' My eyes widened as Heather continued, 'They can't see us but their sense of smell can detect our presence, and their sense of curiosity could pose a challenge.'"

"Wait a second," Jennifer interrupted, "was this just a ruse she was secretly using as, what do you call it, a pattern interrupter?"

"Funny you should ask, because it sure did interrupt my protesting of Heather being harsh and judgmental. I slowly turned around as both of us fell silent and, sure enough, there were two black bear cubs and their mother right outside the pod. We observed them for about thirty seconds, and the cubs joyfully bounced off into the woods with their mother trailing behind, cautiously observing their surroundings and keeping the cubs' desire for mischief at bay.

"After a minute or so, the bears were out of sight, my old pattern had been interrupted, and Heather asked me if I considered myself happy. Normally I would have questioned her intelligence with a rude comment beginning with, 'Uh-*duh!*' but I had gone to the Answer Discovery because I was tired of being angry all the time at everyone who didn't see the world the way I did … which was pretty much everyone.

"I admitted to her that I hadn't been happy in years—maybe decades—since I was a young teenager. Heather ended up saying, 'Good, that's good!' to which I immediately responded, 'How can you say that me not being happy is good?' Heather looked at me with kind eyes and told me that acknowledging that I wasn't where I wanted to be in life was a necessary first step and that my admission was a good thing. She also shared with me that the way I reacted to her saying it was good was proof that change for me isn't easy, that it's a process over time of eliminating old habits and routines that aren't working and substituting new habits and routines specifically designed to get us where we want to be. Then, while acknowledging that change isn't easy, she said four magic words that helped me tremendously: *nothing worthwhile ever is.*

"Something clicked inside my mind when I heard those words, and I realized that I had the ability and the desire to forge a new path for my life that would allow me to live a life that experienced joy, growth, and fulfillment each and every day. It also clicked in my mind *why* what I had previously done as part of my routines and habits wasn't working: They had all been defensive measures designed to protect myself. I had developed a pattern in life of playing not to lose rather than playing to win.

"I was amazed that I had never stepped back and viewed my life as a consultant or life coach would. My self-bias was preventing me from being objective. It was evident now that being righteous, which had led my day from the moment I awoke to the moment I went to sleep, created anger, not joy; created constant frustration, not happiness. Funny, remember the three things we all crave the most each day: appreciation, respect, and love?

"Well, I suddenly realized that I wasn't experiencing *any* of them on a consistent basis, and if I thought I was, I was only fooling myself to avoid the truth. All of this was going through my mind as Heather remained silent and observed me. Finally, sensing that I was making a lot of progress on my own, she brought me back to being in the moment and continuing the path of learning she was walking me down. She explained that the greatest hurdle preventing people from experiencing appreciation, respect, and love on a daily basis was the lack of desire to master the art of forgiveness.

"I remember the feeling of confusion in attempting to reconcile how forgiveness had anything to do with experiencing appreciation, respect, and love, until she explained how important it was for a person to appreciate, respect, and love themselves before they would be able to share with others ... and then have those things returned to them from others. Step one, she said, was to master the art of forgiveness, and the path to mastery began with forgiving oneself."

Jennifer was mesmerized, and her brain was on fire. She saw so much of herself in what Running Bear was revealing in her description of who she was several years ago. The person she described then wasn't anything like the person she perceived was sitting across from her right now. Running Bear continued after taking a long sip of water.

"I felt kind of lost at this point, so I made Heather stop and explain the point she was trying to make more deeply. She began to describe the power of a concept she called 'instantaneous forgiveness,' where when you perceive someone has wronged you, you instantly forgive them, thus eliminating any power the 'wrong' has over you. Whether a spouse, sibling, parent, child, friend, coworker, or someone you don't even know that you encounter on the road, in a store, while on vacation, at work, at a theatre, or at a sporting event … if they do something that ticks you off, or fail to do something you think they should, and it makes you angry, you have just enabled them to have power over you and disabled your ability to continue your pursuit of love, joy, fulfillment, or happiness. She told me I was essentially 'pattern interrupting' myself and my quest for feelings that are good and worthwhile. She helped me identify that I had always tried to maintain a sense of always being in control, of getting everything right, all of the time. This forced me to focus on what was wrong with every other person while totally ignoring what may have been right. I protected myself from ever making a mistake by removing my own vulnerability and never developing trust, the most important part of any relationship. I trusted no one."

"It seems like you were being a little hard on yourself," Jennifer threw out there.

"Which was exactly what I needed at that point if there was any chance I would accept that my life, and how I treated other people, *must* change. If I was being honest, I had to admit to myself that I had hit rock bottom, and had it not been for the Answer Discovery, I'm afraid of where I might have ended up that night. So at this point I knew that how I had been living wasn't giving me what I desired, and I knew *why* what I had been doing wasn't working. It was time for me to say to *myself* 'uh-*duh!*' Anyway, I was certainly intrigued with this concept of 'instantaneous forgiveness,' but I needed a better understanding of how to use it, when to use it, and what I could expect as outcomes if I committed to the use of it.

"Before sharing the 'when' and 'how' of forgiveness, Heather wanted me to understand the reason *why*. She summed it up in one word: love. It's the path of forgiveness that leads to love. Love of spouse, friend, coworker, neighbor, stranger, acquaintance, and others. Forgiveness supports that none of us, *not a single one of us*, is perfect. We all make mistakes. Forgiveness, by us for others and by others for us, keeps us moving down the path of joy, growth, fulfillment, and love. It allows us to give and receive appreciation, respect, and love every day of our lives. And that's what we all crave, isn't it? I've come to realize, with help, mentoring, and support from Heather, that it truly is.

"I remember driving home that evening, arriving about 4:30 a.m. a completely different person. I couldn't sleep even if I wanted to. I sat down at my kitchen table and mapped out a plan of action for change, flowing down the path of forgiveness with the daily destination of appreciation, respect, and love for myself and others. I finished my initial plan at 6:30 a.m., prepared myself for the new day, and have never looked backward since.

"The movie *It's a Wonderful Life* has become my favorite, and one of the best takeaways the movie offers is a saying on a plaque in the office of the main character's father that says, 'The only thing you can take with you is that which you've given away.'

"Since meeting with Heather, I can share that I'm more passionate about helping others than anything else in life. Part of the reason is that I've come to understand even the tiniest compliment can boost someone's self-esteem. You don't even have to know the person. Some of my greatest joy includes seeing a young family in a restaurant and complimenting the parents on their children; never missing an opportunity to thank a veteran for their service to our country; staying after someone's speech to share one way their speech made a positive difference in my thinking; thanking crossing guards, teachers, coaches, custodians, trash haulers, bank tellers … the list goes on.

"I seek to find something right with every person I encounter.

Sometimes I'm shocked to think about how I once used to treat others, but that was in the past, and I accept that had I not fallen so far down, I most likely would never have taken action to climb back up to where I am today."

Running Bear was staring straight into Jennifer's eyes, and Jennifer was returning her stare. Thirty full seconds of silence passed until Jennifer broke the silence with a chuckle and a snort. It was the perfect pattern interrupter for both women. What they had just been through was loaded with intensity, emotion, and passion. Jennifer continued the interruption, saying, "Well, well, well! If I understand this correctly, I was sent here to see you because you were my mirror image about five years ago, you successfully changed who you were, thus experiencing the outcomes that I have shared I desire, and you can help me take a new path that leads me to the place of joy, growth, fulfillment, and love you now find yourself in. Does that about sum it up?"

"It can," RB replied. "But only if you're willing to do what's necessary, with my help, mentoring, and support, to get to the destination where you've told me you want to be living a life of joy, growth, fulfillment, and love that you just mentioned. Today you've been given **The Gift and Power of Forgiveness**. Do you accept this gift and power?"

"I do!" Jennifer exclaimed.

"I'm thankful you used those particular two words, 'I do.' They are often used at moments where a major change in our life is about to occur, where we pledge full commitment. Here is my cell number. It is to be used day or night, when you run into anything from a speed bump to a mountain that's preventing you from moving further down the path we discussed today. Continually remind yourself that anything worthwhile isn't meant to be easy and that all of your positive efforts are rewarded over time. We'll meet here at pod seven one week from today at the same time you arrived today."

The two women hugged, then Jennifer entered her SUV and headed home. She was committed to beginning a whole new life, utilizing the Gift and Power of Forgiveness, and she finally knew *why* staying committed was the only way she could achieve what she truly desired in her heart. It was that precise desire that sent her to the Answer Discovery earlier that day. Now, as she was driving home, she felt completely renewed, wearing a smile so big she could have eaten a banana sideways.

THE GIFT OF
BEING CHOSEN FOR
THE PRIVILEGE

David held the door for his pregnant wife, Amy, as she entered the passenger side of their brand-new minivan. By the time he walked around to the driver's side, he could hear his wife sobbing. He loved her so much. They had been trying to live a fairy tale romance. It all began with a chance meeting involving some miscommunication, a dating period filled with fun and forever memories, both of them scoring dream jobs right out of college, a wedding surrounded by all of the people they loved, the purchase of their first home, and days filled with mostly joy and success over their first three years of marriage.

But their relationship was still evolving, and there were some speed bumps they had had to climb over together—some larger than others. They had their fair share of senseless arguments, but so far, they had managed. However, today they were presented a mountain they had to climb, and both wondered how the other would handle the news they had just received. Some fear began to creep up in Amy's mind as she remembered being asked the question many years ago:

"How many snowflakes does it take to break a branch off a tree?" She overthought what the answer might be until she heard it. The answer was, "One, because up until that point the branch had withstood all the pressure and weight of all of the other snowflakes until that final one had landed." Would the news today be the final snowflake landing on their marriage? She didn't want it to be, but she ended up sobbing over the possibility of losing both her dream of having a normal child and her dream that her marriage would be a special one that would last until "death do us part."

David couldn't stop his mind from racing. Today was different than any other day and appeared to pose the most difficult challenge any couple could ever face. David got in the van, reached out for his wife's hand, and began sobbing himself as he intertwined his fingers in hers. He wanted to be strong, both for himself and the woman with whom he had proclaimed, "I do, for richer or poorer, in sickness and in health, till death do us part." He just didn't think those vows would be tested until they had grown old together. David's mind was all over the place and out of control. Through the crying, he suddenly realized that he had just repeated the words, "What are we going to do?" out loud. He hadn't meant for his wife to hear those words—clearly he was losing control of his emotions.

It was actually Amy who began to calm her sobbing down, concerned about its possible impact on the life that was growing inside her. While attempting to get her breathing under control, she managed to say, "It's best that we let each other cry through our current emotions." She paused, taking in a deep breath through her nose and slowly blowing the breath out through her mouth with her lips pursed together. She repeated the process, then continued, "We have a lot to discuss and a lot to educate ourselves about regarding what we were just told, followed up by developing a plan and strategy of how to move forward."

Amy had always been thankful that her math minor in college had, more than anything, taught her to think logically, approach challenges with a step-by-step process, and create a strategy that led to the desired solution.

As Amy was attempting to rein in her emotions, her husband seemed to be succumbing to the fear and sadness that had moved to the forefront of his mind. Amy breathed deeply a third time, then glanced over at her husband. She loved this man so much. They had discovered a love for each other that, on most days, had proven to be so much deeper than the "happily ever after" love portrayed in fairy tales and Hallmark movies. Although their love for each other was being tested, Amy firmly believed that they could successfully navigate *any* challenge to that love, including the challenge placed in front of them today. Amy vowed not to let this be the one snowflake that would end their relationship. She reminded herself of the foundation for their marriage that they had been so careful in creating. She believed that foundation to be solid.

She began to get her crying under control, looked at her husband, and proclaimed, "I need a hug!" Knowing what that meant, and without even glancing back at Amy, David began an attempt to control his breathing, grabbed the door latch, opened the door, stepped outside the vehicle, closed the door, and began to walk around to the other side of the van. Meanwhile, Amy had exited the van and watched her husband as he approached her. She ever so slightly smiled when she looked at David, completely understanding the emotions that had transferred to his face and his eyes. David was having a hard time allowing his eyes to meet Amy's, but he knew she wouldn't mind. What was most important right now was what was about to occur.

They embraced … and it was the kind that occurred when a person embraced someone they loved deeply but hadn't seen in over a decade—one you might see at an airport or family reunion. Once their courtship had taken off, Amy and David spent an entire after-noon analyzing the word *hug* and the unique power it offered. It had been an afternoon filled with laughter as they debated different hug-ging techniques and then tried them out for analysis. They experi-mented with hugs that kind of felt creepy, lean-in hugs that seemed respectful, side hugs which seemed best used for acquaintances and buddy-type friends, hugging from behind (which neither of them liked receiving), and long-lost friend and family hugs.

As fun as that afternoon was, in the end they realized they had gained a powerful tool, fully recognizing the power that a hug, if per-formed correctly, could have. Since their discovery, hugs had become part of their daily ritual with each other. It morphed into one of them saying, "I need a hug" or even just the word "hug." When either of these occurred—which they did two to three times per day—they would pause, wrap their arms fully around each other, nest their necks while resting their chins on each other's shoulder, and melt into the embrace, letting it linger until the two felt they were standing there as one. That was what was occurring right now outside their min-ivan in the parking lot of the building they had just had an ultra-sound performed at.

Both had a moment where they lost the battle with the emotions causing the crying, and so they embraced just a little bit tighter. The embrace was just getting to the point where they both felt like a child being hugged by a parent, realizing it's all going to be okay, when it happened. David was so deep into sending and receiving love that he lost his balance for a second, went to shift his foot to regain bal-ance, and stepped squarely on Amy's left toes.

"OW!" Amy exclaimed, wondering why she had chosen sandals that day.

"Oh no, I'm so sorry, honey. I didn't mean to do that. Here, let me kiss it and make it better." David dropped to his knees, lifted

Amy's foot, and began kissing her toes. Amy first looked down, then looked around, and noticed three other people who were witnessing what David was doing.

Amy looked down at her husband and let out a little chuckle, saying, "David … my fruitcake husband … I'm fine. It really didn't hurt at all, but I was so filled with emotion I think it gave me an opportunity to shed a little of it when I said 'ow.' It's turning out to be such an incredible interruption that I'm glad you did it. Let's get back in the van, head to our favorite tea lounge, and see if we can't talk this through and process what we've been told."

David looked in his wife's eyes with complete gratitude that *this* was the woman he was married to and said, "Hug," knowing that she was the only other person in the world at that moment who would know how much that single word meant to him. They embraced again and held it for a full thirty seconds. Then they got into their new minivan and headed to one of their favorite places: the Blue Sapphire Tea Lounge.

By the time they arrived, their eyes weren't quite so red anymore, and they had begun to communicate about what they had been told and discuss a potential strategy that could lead them to a decision about what to do. Amy headed over toward a table in a vacant corner and fired up her tablet, which automatically connected to the Wi-Fi. Then she took out her wireless mouse and keyboard and glanced over to see her husband bringing over her decaf Essence tea, along with his favorite, a simple vanilla latte.

"Wow, that was fast."

"Isn't it awesome, especially on a day like today?" David responded. "One of the benefits of being loyal to a business and appreciating their incredible service and products. They saw us pulling in and had our drinks ready by the time I stepped up to the counter."

David sat down and, after they both took a much-needed sip

of their drinks, looked lovingly over at Amy. Noticing his stare, her eyes came up from the screen placed in front of both of them and met his look.

"I do," said Amy.

"I do," said David.

Funny, isn't it, how some couples develop a form of communication where thousands of words worth of feelings, emotions, and love can be reduced to a simple look or a couple of words? Out of all the words spoken on their wedding day, the most important to each of them were the two simple words, "I do." Throughout the more than three years they had been married, they had been diligent about consistently using the words "I do" at the most unlikely of times. It may not have been daily, but it was close. For each of them it signified the deep love they had for each other and how committed they were, no matter what, to loving each other "til death do they part." They both realized that their commitment to the words "I do" had rarely been tested. Until today, that is. While this caused a bit of anxiety inside both of them—anxiety that they weren't ready to share with one another—they had both been raised with a "soldier on" kind of mentality.

Amy looked over at David and asked, "Ready?" After getting the nod from David, they both turned their attention to the screen, where Amy typed into the search engine two words: "Down syndrome." Both Amy and David were instantly overwhelmed. The amount of information, along with all of the pictures of people who looked different, was coming at them at a speed that they were struggling to handle. Both began to tear up again. Right at that moment, Phyliss, the manager of the Blue Sapphire Tea Lounge, came up behind David and Amy and placed a small plate with a warm blueberry scone, cut in half with two small forks on either side, on the table right between them.

"You two come here on a regular basis, and we're so fortunate that you do," she said. "That scone is fresh out of the oven and is on the house. You both look like you could use a dose of 'down home happy' and…"

Right then Phyliss's eyes went to the screen and saw the pictures of people with Down syndrome, with different URLs all pointing to information about the condition.

"Hey, Down syndrome. Are you two checking up on our favorite employee, Adam?" The blank stares coming back to Phyliss from both David and Amy indicated otherwise.

"You know who I'm talking about, right? Haven't you noticed him when you've been in here before? Huh … looking at your faces, I guess not. He's such a big personality here, we all kinda assume he's a hard guy to miss. Sorry, I didn't mean to … oh my goodness. You're both crying. Something's wrong." Phyliss moved around to the other side of the four-top table and sat across from Amy and David. "I swear, the only reason I'm manager at this place is because I'm a really good listener. Anything you'd like to share with me?"

Amy and David looked at each other and knew. They were both trying to be brave and strong but struggling as they were faced with something neither of them had any experience with. David looked at Phyliss and said, "Amy is five months pregnant and earlier today had an ultrasound. Our doctor wanted us to wait until she could read the results and told us they saw some abnormalities that would indicate our baby will be born with Down syndrome."

Phyliss's face immediately took on a look of compassion and love. "And?…"

Amy chimed in, "And we came here to calm down and do some research on what this means for all the plans we've made preparing to start a family."

"I'm so glad you chose to come here," Phyliss said. "I have a lot of experience with Adam, and I'd like to offer you both a suggestion. When Adam's parents found out their second child had Down syndrome, they went to this place called the Answer Discovery. They tell other people that that single decision to visit the Answer Discovery led them down a path to the most wonderful life they had ever envisioned. As Adam's manager I'm so thankful that their path included sharing Adam with us five days a week. I think educating yourself with data and research is a wonderful strategy, but it's our emotions that guide us through our most challenging times. Might I suggest you visit the Answer Discovery first and then let your research fall into place? You may end up researching from a totally different perspective if you do."

David and Amy looked at each other, looked at Phyliss, then looked back at each other and knew: They liked this new strategy. It provided the opportunity to lift what was on their shoulders and toss it off for at least a short while. Phyliss had just offered an opportunity for them to regroup and rethink. They thanked Phyliss for the advice and said they would visit the Answer Discovery as soon as they finished that wonderful scone she had just delivered. With that, Phyliss stood up and headed back to the kitchen, and Amy and David both enjoyed their first bite of what they would remember as the best scone they would ever eat.

While neither Amy nor David had ever been to the Answer Discovery, they knew where it was and had heard a few stories about it. It seemed like a really good thing to do as they continued to try to manage their emotions. Maybe they could finish the day with some peace of mind and of heart. They both agreed that would be a good way to finish. After they finished eating the best scone ever and bussed their mugs, forks, and plate over to the washstand, they waved to Phyliss, who stuck her head out of the kitchen, smiled, and wished them good luck.

Before starting the minivan engine, David looked at Amy and gently said, "I do." Amy returned the look and sweetly said, "I do." Then Amy searched for "Answer Discovery" with her map app, and they were on their way. When the couple exited the structure later that day, they had smiles and a genuine look of contentment on their faces. David spoke first.

"Never in my life have I had an experience like the one we just had. Nothing even close."

"Yeah … same here," Amy chimed in. "Funny isn't it? As strange as it was, I never once felt afraid. In fact, the emotions that took the place of the fear I had when I entered with were feelings of compassion, calmness, openness, caring, respect. In the strangest of ways, I felt loved the entire time we were in there. Love not only for the both of us, but loving sensitivity to the situation we find ourselves in. I'm so thankful that we have twenty-four hours before we meet Sue and Duke. The twenty-four-hour rule gives us an opportunity to put our current emotions in park before making a decision. To be honest, I'm emotionally spent right now, and I surmise you're in the same place."

"Kind of cool that we meet them right back at Blue Sapphire Tea Lounge and that tomorrow is Saturday, so neither of us has to take additional time off work. Two in the afternoon is perfect. Hey, honey—my one true love—how about we pick up a pizza on the way home and watch some old musical that finishes with a happy ending?" David opened the passenger door for his wife as she slid into the seat. Her pregnancy was beginning to show, and she reclined the back of the seat just a little more to find the perfect comfort spot.

As David began to close her door, Amy asked, "And can we also stop and get an extra jar of…." The door had closed, and David hadn't heard the last word, but he smiled, knowing that the last word was "pickles." His wife had developed a strange obsession with pickles that she never had before she was pregnant. He chuckled to himself as he rounded the van to the driver's side and thought about how strange it was that she had wanted him to buy a jar of pickles at the exact same time he was purchasing a pregnancy test kit that would soon indicate they were going to be parents.

They pulled away from the curb and headed to the only pizza place they knew that had jars of pickles in the same cooler as the two-liter bottles of soda. Together, they were already experiencing the calming effects that the wonderful twenty-four-hour rule offered them. The pizza, movie, and even the pickles had fulfilled the intentions they had been pursued for.

David and Amy ended up watching the classic film *Seven Brides for Seven Brothers*, singing along with the songs they had committed to memory after watching it at least ten previous times over the five years they had been seeing each other. In fact, it was the very first movie they had watched together. As they went to bed, having the information their doctor had given them still fresh in their minds, they prayed together for the first time in a long time. Just two weeks prior they had had a discussion about what role faith would play in their lives, now that they were adding a child. They hadn't come to any conclusions but agreed they needed to come up with a plan to join some type of church and figure out the role it would play as their child grew.

Praying as they lay in bed just seemed like a good thing to do. They prayed for themselves, for their unborn child, and for the hope of getting restful sleep that night after what had been an unsettling day. Unfortunately, their 'restful sleep' praying was not answered with success. Cold, hot, bad dreams, snoring by one and then the other, thirst, bathroom breaks … By 6:00 a.m. they both gave up and got out of bed. As they did, both of them opened the flood gates of their eyes back up while melting into each other's arms. They didn't let go of each other until Amy muttered, "My bladder's about to burst, so if we don't let go of each other we may need to put on some waterproof slippers." Her comment broke the tension, and they both laughed as David quickly released his bear hug and Amy headed for the bathroom.

David headed for the kitchen and began to prepare their favorite steel-cut oatmeal. He glanced at the calendar Amy had created and noted that this would be the thirty-seventh day that she had eaten oatmeal for breakfast. While he let out a little chuckle, he couldn't help but think how proud he was of his wife, who had done extensive research on what food is best when pregnant for both the unborn child and the mother. He felt so lucky to be married to a woman whom he admired for attempting to do everything right in preparation for the birth of their first child.

* * *

When Amy and David entered the Blue Sapphire Tea Lounge, they first noticed Phyliss working behind the counter. They had arrived fifteen minutes early, as they acknowledged that today they were cautiously concerned about not only everything that had happened in the last twenty-four hours, but also about what they were about to hear from a couple they didn't even know. As they took a few steps toward the counter, they glanced to their left, noticing a young man cleaning one of the decorated mirrors on the wall when he suddenly, upon finishing, stepped back and, looking directly at himself in the mirror, exclaimed, "Hello, handsome!"

Phyliss laughed without even looking up. "Okay, Mr. Handsome, how about you pause on the personal admiration and keep cleaning?" As David and Amy came up to the counter, Phyliss smiled at them and said, "People wonder why we love Adam so much, and you just witnessed one of our favorite reasons. He has such high self-esteem. I mean, how many people do you know could get away with a wisecrack like, 'Hello, handsome' and not have people think less of them? It's just one more reason that we feel it's a privilege to have him on our team. We've come to understand this unique feeling of betterment, commonly referred to as the 'Adam Effect,' which is something I think you're going to learn a lot more about today when you meet with Duke and Sue."

Right then, both Amy and David looked over at this young man, and it wasn't until they looked closer that they realized he had Down syndrome. When they let their stare linger, they noticed something attached to his belt with thin tubing coming out of it that was then tucked into his pants. As they met each other's eyes, they both attempted to hide a look of concern, not knowing what it was nor what it meant. Right at that moment Phyliss told them that Duke and Sue were waiting for them in the lounge's most popular room, the Room of Caring. Amy and David had heard of the room, and knew where it was, but they had never gone into it over the many times they had frequented the Blue Sapphire.

"Why do you call it the Room of Caring?" inquired David.

"Because that's what the sign says above the door of the entrance," Phyliss replied with a smile. "And I think you'll understand more of the reason why after your meeting today. I just had the same drinks you ordered yesterday taken back there, and you'll find some comfort food offerings and some bottles of water. I'll check on all of you every so often in case you need anything else. Thanks for coming here today."

Amy and David headed toward what would become a defining moment in their relationship and in both of their lives. As they entered the Room of Caring, both of them were attempting to form first impressions based on what they immediately noticed. Both David and Amy noticed that Duke and Sue appeared to be happy, healthy, in their mid-forties, well-groomed in comfortable-looking casual wear, and both noticed that, when Duke and Sue stood up to welcome them, Sue appeared to be about six feet tall—slightly taller than Duke. Amy and David didn't really have much choice with the method of introduction, as Duke and Sue immediately gave each of them a warm and welcome hug.

The first words both Sue and Duke shared were a simultaneous, "Congratulations! We're so happy for you!" Sue continued, "Welcome to the club we refer to as Those Chosen for the Privilege. We're excited to open up and share our life with you and provide some answers, some love, some thought processes, and some opportunities for the two of you to have a positive impact on our community." As the four of them sat down, David and Amy felt the rush of the inevitable anxiety that they had been feeling all morning begin to melt away. Duke began to speak.

"Sue and I have been brought up to speed on what's happening right now in your life, and we'd like to begin by saying that even though we've just met, we care deeply about you, your future family, and your family's future. If you're willing to accept our commitment, we're willing to commit to you both, to be there when you need us and to help you with decisions you will be asked to make that fall outside the traditional parenting decisions."

Sue continued, "We commit to being the type of people that will hold your hand without being judgmental in *all* of your decisions regarding your relationship with each other, additional children you may have, your immediate family members, and your friends and neighbors." Sue paused for a few seconds, then slowly said, "*It's critically important that you both know that everything is going to be okay.*" Then she paused again, allowing that to sink in. "You can both take a deep breath now and settle in to what the next couple of hours holds for all of us. Every couple we know that has been placed in the same situation you find yourself in has lots of questions. But first we'd like to relate a story that someone shared with us right after Adam was born. It had a huge, I mean really huge, impact on the way we approached this journey we've embraced and been rewarded with."

Duke was about to begin the story, but he lingered for a moment on the last part of the sentence Sue had just said and, smiling, he softly repeated the words,

"'This journey we've embraced and been rewarded with.' Wow! That's just so blatantly true and so very awesome. Right after Adam was born and we found out he had an extra chromosome on his twenty-first pair, we found ourselves at the Answer Discovery. We were sent to meet with a couple that shared with us what life would be like moving forward. They paraphrased a poem written by Emily Perl Kingsley, entitled 'Welcome to Holland,' and they told it something like this:

"For years a young couple had nurtured a dream of going to Italy. They saved their money and educated themselves on all that Italy had to offer. They wanted it all, and so they did research on the Colosseum, the works of Michelangelo, and the gondolas in Venice. They purchased 'how to speak Italian' programs along with guidebooks. They were finally ready and prepared for the trip of a lifetime. With their bags checked at the airport, they boarded the plane that would take them to Italy. After several hours of flying, the plane finally landed. The couple's excitement was at its peak, knowing their dream was about to begin, when the captain of the plane announced on the public address system, 'Welcome to Holland.'

"'Holland?!' they asked. 'What do you mean, Holland? We signed up for Italy! We're supposed to be in Italy. For years we've dreamed of going to Italy.' But unbeknownst to them, there had been a change in the flight plan. They had landed in Holland, and there they must stay."

Then Sue took over the reins. "This is where they almost lost us, because they injected a story within a story to make the ultimate point.

They told us that there was an old Native American lesson that was passed down from generation to generation. It began with an elder teaching that each day, when we awake from sleep, we have a wolf on each side of us. On one side of us the wolf is a Positive Wolf, which can guide us through everything that will occur that day with a *positive* perspective. On the other side of us is a Negative Wolf, which can guide us through everything that will occur that day with a *negative* perspective. The two wolves will fight for our attention. The winner will dominate our day with its guidance. We cannot wake up without both of these foes being present, but we can determine which one will guide us each day by whichever one we feed the most. The one we feed quickly grows stronger and can quickly defeat the other, leaving the rest of the day to guide us with the chosen perspective. The most important part of this lesson is that we—each of us—get to *choose* which one we feed, which will then ultimately determine the outcomes of our day. Which wolf will you feed?" Sue looked over at Duke and asked, "Honey, would you like to tie it all together?"

Duke took over, saying,

"The point is that all of us get to choose, regarding everything in life. Do we react or respond? There's a big difference. The couple that had put so much planning into Italy now find themselves in Holland, without an option to visit Italy at this time. So what will they do? They have to choose. They can react or respond.

"If they react, it looks like this: They spend every moment for the next two weeks of their life suffering. They battle with the airline, making demands to refund their money, cover all their costs, and pay for other modes of transportation to get them to Italy in an attempt to salvage at least part of their dream. All to no avail. They'll be able to cry and whine to all of their family and friends, and anyone else who will listen, as to how they were wronged and what a horrible experience it turned out to be.

"ORRRRR they could respond. They could respond by acknowledging that Holland wasn't what they signed up for, but it's precisely where they find themselves for the next two weeks. They could support the thought that Italy could still occur at some time in the future, and they would have that to look forward to. Then they could immerse themselves in the possibility of Holland being an adventure—an adventure that could possibly turn out to be the greatest adventure they might ever experience.

"You see, when they landed in Holland and were told they must stay, they each had a wolf sitting on each of their sides. Which wolf would they choose to feed? Whichever wolf they fed was going to determine whether the next two weeks of their life would be their biggest shared disaster or possibly their greatest shared adventure.

"That decision would also play a *huge* role in every future decision they would make as a couple for the rest of their lives. Decisions regarding their love for each other, the strength of their marriage, their parenting preferences, the way they viewed family and friends, caring for their aging parents someday, the role work was to play in their life, the role they would play in their neighborhood and the community they lived in, and the role the community would play in *their* lives. That one decision made on the plane in Holland could eventually crumble every part of the life they were building together *or* it could create a foundation of love for each other that nothing … *nothing* could ever crack nor damage."

Right as Duke finished that sentence, there was a knock at the door that slightly startled the four. They all glanced at the glass door to see Adam's smiling face. Sue motioned him in, and Adam backed through the door towing an elegant cart with a large bowl of cut-up mixed fruit, four bowls with forks for the fruit, and some refills for the drinks that they all had. Once inside, Adam turned and faced his parents and this new couple, smiled wide, and said with enthusiasm,

"At your service!" Duke followed that with, "Adam, you are the biggest ham I know!" to which Adam responded in his best fake British accent, "Right so, Guv'nor!" Sue, Duke, and Adam all chuckled as Sue just shook her head side to side, enjoying the moment. David and Amy were taking all of this in and appreciated the opportunity to witness the three interacting with each other. Later, they would refer to this moment as one that helped in transitioning their thoughts to the possibility of embracing the positive wolf in the face of this new and different adventure they now found themselves on.

Adam cleared the cups and dishes that had already been used, wiped the table with a damp disinfectant wipe, and placed the fresh drinks and fruit on the table the four of them were sitting at. They all said, "Thank you," to which Adam responded, "My pleasure." As he exited, he paused, turned toward the four of them, smiled, and said, "Bonjour!"

Sue finally resumed the conversation the four adults were having. "We found great value in our meeting with the couple the Answer Discovery connected us with. We were so fortunate to have had the Answer Discovery set it up at the moment we needed it the most. They helped us decide which wolf would dominate our lives each and every day. Always choosing the Positive Wolf has blessed us with an incredible life that we might have missed out on if it hadn't been for their love, compassion, perspective, and guidance. That's why we feel so great about meeting here with you today. We know you have a lot of questions, and we're ready to be open and honest with you, so tell us what those questions are."

Both Amy and David noticed that Sue and Duke had smiles on their faces. Warm smiles. Friendly smiles. It really appeared that they were comfortable, confident, and really eager to help. That alone was helpful. Amy let go with the first question: "Did you know beforehand that you were going to have a child with Down syndrome?"

Duke responded, "No, and I have to admit we weren't thrilled with the way we were told. Adam was our second child. With our knowledge and experience of the birth of our first son, and the fact that we only lived a mile and a half from the hospital, we ended up waiting a little too long at home when Sue's contractions got closer together. Forty-five minutes after we arrived at the hospital, Sue experienced a beautiful natural birth, and Adam came into the world. The doctor hadn't made it to the hospital yet, and an angel of a nurse delivered Adam. It was so amazing to witness the childbirth miracle a second time. We were full of joy. Adam was born around two in the afternoon, and we were prepared to take him home later that day."

Sue took over the story. "We became concerned when they told us they wanted to keep him overnight, and then a parade of medical people kept coming in to examine him, saying nothing to us when they did. It seemed like there was a concern, but no one would share anything with us. They kept telling us everything was fine. The three of us stayed at the hospital overnight. We woke up the next morning and prepared to be sent home."

Duke kicked back in. "We were told that they needed the doctor to sign a release. Our normal doctor was on vacation at the time, and one of his partners was supposed to come in to release us. Sue was receiving meals through the hospital, but when it looked like the doctor wouldn't arrive until well after noon, I told Sue I was going to grab a sandwich down at the hospital cafeteria. I was only gone about twenty minutes, and when I came back to the room, Sue was in tears, holding Adam. I ran up to her and asked what was wrong, and she said, 'The doctor came by and told me they think he has Down syndrome.' I embraced my wife and our new son and whispered to her that our son had been blessed with the best parents in the world, and we were going to take great care of him whether he had Down syndrome or not."

Sue continued, "It was such a pivotal moment in our life and in our marriage, signifying that we both were willing to accept the news we'd just received and that we were committed to having it make our marriage and life together even stronger and amplify the desire to be the best parents in the world to this new addition to our family."

Duke shared, "The only thing that was upsetting to me at that moment was that the doctor didn't even ask Sue where her husband was; he told her when she was alone with Adam." Duke had to pause for a moment. "I was right there in the hospital, and he could have waited for me to return if he had just asked, and we could have received the news together. He was obviously uncomfortable sharing the news, but because he wasn't our regular doctor, he didn't really know us. I remember making a vow to Sue that I wanted to do whatever we could so that any couple in the future didn't ever have to worry about receiving news about a newborn in the way we experienced."

David looked at Duke and asked, "Did you ever end up doing anything?"

Sue responded, "We sure did. A few months later we helped create a program in which anytime a child was delivered at our hospital with what they suspected, or knew, was Down syndrome, Duke and I would be contacted, and we would as quickly as possible come over to the hospital and meet with the parents or mother before they were released from the hospital. We developed a lot of close friendships with other people who eventually joined the Those Chosen for the Privilege club we mentioned earlier. When HIPAA laws came into play, the hospital could no longer notify us directly. The only thing they could do was share our contact information with the parents of the newborn. Our ability to help others experiencing a child born with Down syndrome significantly decreased. Then we realized that the Answer Discovery had provided us with the angels we needed, so we went to the Answer Discovery and requested the opportunity to help others as we had at the hospital. Pretty soon we started receiving notifications from the Answer Discovery every time someone came in with questions regarding Down syndrome, which is what led the two of you to the two of us today."

"That's twice you've mentioned this club you refer to as 'Those Chosen for the Privilege,' and I'm curious what you mean by that," said Amy.

Sue smiled and said, "By the time you leave here today, it will be very clear what that club represents and how you, too, can be members. If it isn't crystal clear, then we have failed, and failure with any of us in our family isn't an option. We believe that it can never be called 'failure' unless someone gives up. We will never give up. Never! Including attempting to help you and others like you."

"Thanks, Sue. So what are the things can we expect?" asked Amy.

Sue continued, "When we had our first child, we found great value in reading a book entitled *What to Expect When You're Expecting*. It really helped prepare us for the things we needed to know to begin parenting with success."

David interrupted Sue, saying, "It's funny you mention that book. Amy and I are both in the process of reading it and love how it's preparing us. But this is going to be different, isn't it? I mean with the Down syndrome and all…."

Both Duke and Sue could see the forlorn look becoming prominent on the faces across from them. Sue, in a compassionate and loving way, continued. "You can expect your child with Down syndrome to be 99 percent the same as any child. They smile, they eat, they cry when they need something, they sleep, they fill diaper…"—Duke held his nose when his wife mentioned *that* one—"…they bring you great love and joy, they interrupt your sleep, they make you childproof your home, and they steal your heart. Their fingernails and toenails will need trimming, their hair will grow along with their body. They'll crave your touch and your love. They'll jump when they hear the sound of your voice. They'll make sounds that you'll attempt to imitate."

David interrupted Sue again, not intending to be rude, but as a result of some anxiety that was beginning to build up. "We're pretty comfortable with all that stuff. We're more concerned with what will be different." Duke and Sue glanced at each other and gently smiled, knowing that it was one of the indicators they had been waiting for. They had learned it was best to let the people they were mentoring bring up the elephant in the room, indicating they had at least attempted to prepare themselves for what they might hear in response.

Both David and Amy reached for some of the additional snacks that were sitting in front of them—Amy because she was still hungry after eating the mixed fruit, and David because eating helped calm him in stressful situations. They smiled at each other, having reached for the food at the exact same time.

Sue knew that Duke always liked handling this one. He began, "When someone has a child with Down syndrome, their life is about to change ... but I hate to utilize the word *change* because when nearly everyone hears it, they believe that the change will automatically be negative. What Sue and I have done, utilizing the Positive Wolf each day, is substitute the word *improve* for the word *change*. Your life is about to *improve*. Our current society will always default to the word *change* when they look at or meet your child with Down syndrome. Their initial focus will automatically zoom in on the 1 percent of your child that's different rather than the 99 percent that's just like every other child. Funny how small children don't notice any differences in things like skin color, hairstyle, eye shape, nor disability, but from about first grade on through adult, people do. In your future you'll find yourself caring more about other people—not so much what they think, but you'll want them to see your child the way you do. You'll want to share the incredible benefits that you've gained by being blessed with a child with disabilities that other people haven't been given the opportunity to discover. Benefits like becoming a better listener and a more compassionate, loving, and caring person. Benefits like massively celebrating the smallest of successes, knowing that they represent positive movement toward a long-term goal. Benefits like seeing all things in a much simpler way with a clearer vision of what's really important in this world. Having a child with Down syndrome gives both of you an incredible opportunity to bring positive change to our community and to the world. You can be part of the greater good if you choose to share what you will experience with others whenever an opportunity presents itself."

"Will everyone we share this with be willing to understand and accept our point of view? I'm not sure I'd be comfortable trying to change the world right now," Amy said.

"Right." Duke continued, "Takes me back to my sales training when I learned SW-SW-SW-N."

David interrupted, "Which means?"

"Some Will, Some Won't, So What, Next. You're both on a path to becoming a professional seed planter, and the seeds you'll be planting are seeds that, when properly nurtured, can lead to a better life for anyone you plant them with. All Sue and I are really doing here today with the two of you is planting an abundant amount of seeds and providing you with the necessary water, fertilizer, and tools to make those seeds grow to become incredible."

There was a slight pause that David broke with, "Wow. You two are a little overwhelming. I'm not sure we could ever be like you."

"Duke and I would agree with you," Sue countered. "We both firmly believe that the two of you will *far* exceed what we have achieved, and we're willing to commit to help get you there. At a conference one day, the speaker asked, 'When is an apple tree successful?' I was the first to raise my hand and answer, 'Easy, when it produces apples.' I was quickly told that I was incorrect. I had been so sure of that answer, but when the speaker shared that 'an apple tree is successful when it produces *other apple trees*,' I immediately understood the point she was making. Just producing apples means that once the tree stops, it loses all of its value to the world. But if the *seeds* from the apples it produces create additional apple trees that in turn create even more, then the goodness of that original tree lives on forever. It's kind of the same with the lessons we humans share with each other. The goal is for each new generation to surpass the awesomeness of the one that preceded it and for its positive influence to spread and grow."

Amy and David were really tuning in to what they were hearing. They had established a comfort level with Duke and Sue and had so much more they wanted to ask and so much more they hoped they would learn. Amy shifted gears and asked, "What else can we expect?"

Sue looked at Duke and asked him, "Okay if I take this one?" Duke smiled and gave her a wink of his left eye with a twinkle in his right. "You're going to face a lot of choices that many couples who don't ever have a child with disabilities never have to face. Current statistics show the average divorce rate is about 45 percent. When you add a child with disabilities to a marriage, the divorce rate jumps to over 75 percent. Interestingly enough, the couples that make up the 25 percent of marriages that remain intact after having a child with disabilities discover a level of relationship that few other couples ever enjoy. Here's the reason: The emotions you experience while raising a child with disabilities are enhanced with more complete understanding. That enhanced emotion runs over into your relationship with your spouse because you're experiencing it *together*. It also runs over into the relationship you have with your other children. Your marriage and your family have a unique advantage over every other family if that's how you choose to see it."

Duke jumped in at this point and said, "It might help if I share a story that supports what Sue just shared. A television station was creating a special presentation about people with disabilities, and they approached us to see if we'd participate. We've always been willing to share with others, so it was only natural that we'd embrace the opportunity. The program was attempting to examine the *difference* in the way each parent processed having a child with disabilities. When we showed up, they led us to separate rooms to be individually interviewed. One of the questions Sue and I were both asked was "What's the greatest gift you've ever received?" Without hesitation, we both answered, "Having a child with disabilities!" Neither of us knew that we'd be asked that question, nor did we immediately know how the other person responded to it. After the interviews, when we first saw each other, we were both jumping over each other's words attempting to tell each other how we had responded to that particular question. When we realized that both of us had responded with the exact same words, we laughed out loud, looked each other in the eyes, gave each other the greatest embrace humankind has ever known, and wept. That moment had added a whole new level of blocks to the foundation of our marriage, our relationship, and to each of our lives."

At this point, Sue and Duke looked at each other as tears began to form in their eyes. They simultaneously said the word "hug," then stood up and embraced each other in a way that broadcast their deep love for each other. It was a thing of beauty to witness, and David and Amy found themselves reaching for each other's hand and squeezing it just enough to indicate that they, too, wanted to continue to try to love each other deeply. They smiled at the odd coincidence of Sue and Duke saying "hug" just like they did and sharing a warm embrace.

"During those separate interviews, we were also asked how we felt about the push in many Scandinavian countries to eliminate *all* Down syndrome births through testing and abortions. We both responded how sad it made us. When they asked why it made us sad, we were once again united in our response, both going back to how we answered the 'greatest gift we had ever received' question. We couldn't imagine that someone might want to destroy potentially the most precious and valuable gift they would ever receive, just because other members of society, including the vast majority of doctors in the world, think that the child they had conceived is less than perfect. We also shared our frustration with the fact that the advice and opinion that was being pushed on the citizens of those Scandinavian countries was being given by people who had never themselves experienced a family member with disabilities and the rewards, benefits, and blessings that accompany the experience."

You could have heard a pin drop. This was obviously an emotional subject for Duke and Sue, and it was slowly becoming one for Amy and David. Prior to getting pregnant they had talked about their views on abortion, and both of them indicated to each other that they weren't comfortable with abortion being part of their life on this earth. They had hoped they could skirt the issue by never being placed in a circumstance that required them to make such a difficult decision, but hoping doesn't always work. Just yesterday their doctor had said it was an option they should consider and that they would need to make a decision as soon as possible if they intended to abort the child that was growing inside of Amy. Duke and Sue both knew that Amy and David had been given that option and had successfully shared their thoughts without trying to push David and Amy in a corner. They recognized the free will we all have to make our own decisions, and they were comfortable sharing what led them to the decisions that, in turn, led them to feel blessed beyond compare.

David had another question. "We noticed coming in that your son had what looked like a unique kind of cell phone on his belt, and it looked like there was a thin plastic tube coming out of it."

"Ahh, yes," Sue responded. "Adam's pancreas stopped producing insulin twenty years ago, right after his second birthday. He's a type-1 diabetic. What you saw was his insulin pump. Both Duke and I agree that managing his Down syndrome has produced a lot less anxiety than his diabetes. Having said that, Adam's diabetes has offered us many lessons in life that have helped shape our compassion and care for all other people on this earth. It's helped us to attempt to never judge others. We always attempt to learn through the strength of other people's character. We would both admit that it has been challenging all these years to invoke the Positive Wolf, turning Adam's diabetes into a blessing, but our perspective continues to view it as a gift."

Sue gently continued the discussion as their time together that day was winding down.

"Adam finishes his shift soon, and we'd like to provide an opportunity for both of you to get to know him. He'll join us here shortly. We'd also like to meet with you a few more times before your child arrives and many times after. We'd also like to introduce you to The Arc, which is an advocate group for all people with developmental and intellectual disabilities. Their help and support, along with the educational and networking opportunities, have been instrumental in our family's dynamics and success. We have so much to share with you that will help both of you in all the phases of raising a child, including some that you will experience having a child with disabilities that others won't experience.

"Before Adam joins us, we have a story we'd like to share that will explain the adventure our family has been enjoying since the day Adam was born. The fact that having Adam as a son and family member was an incredibly awesome adventure hadn't really hit home with us until Adam was in the eighth grade and a member of the football team during his final year at middle school.

"But I should begin with how we approached school. Believing that special education was a service and not a place, we chose to have Adam fully included in the regular classroom with his peers from his very first year in preschool when he was three years old. Gradually we learned how to help and support the teachers that were willing to try having a child with disabilities in their classroom, rather than the special ed classroom. While we ran into some hurdles, speed bumps, and walls we had to get around, by the time Adam finished third grade, we realized the positive impact Adam was having on his classmates, his teacher, and other people associated with the school, including the custodian, principal, and office staff.

"As we learned and fine-tuned our approach to Adam's school experience, we realized he kept impacting more and more people in our community because he was fully included in school, in Cub Scouts and later Boy Scouts, in community sports teams, in our church's youth group program, and in everything else his older brother had been involved in, just like his younger brothers would eventually experience.

"In the fall of his eighth-grade year he was on the football team. The head coach, Coach Ched, one of the finest human beings we know, had a special relationship with Adam. At the time Adam could pump out more perfect push-ups than 90 percent of the rest of the team. He utilized Adam's attitude and commitment to consistently seek improvement each and every day as an example for the other players to look up to."

Duke suddenly blurted out, "Oh please, please, please, please, please, can I take over the story?"

Sue shook her head and laughed. "Oh my goodness, you are so dramatic. Yes, dear, you can take over."

Both David and Amy could really sense the love these two people they had just met had for each other. Duke, with great excitement, continued the story. "Remember Sue mentioned that during Adam's eighth-grade football season, we both realized that having a child with disabilities was an incredibly awesome adventure? Here's what triggered it. In the middle of the season we were approached by the local news organization, which had caught wind of Adam being fully included on the middle school football team, and they wanted to do a story on Adam. After asking a few questions we declined the offer, believing that they just wanted to do a feel-good story about Adam. We had been trying to raise our kids to be humble and to understand that life *isn't about 'me, me, me.'* Plus, we believed that the real story was so much bigger than that. We spent a lot of time talking about this around the kitchen table. Our oldest son was a tenth grader in high school, and he shared what we had decided and why with one of his buddies who just happened to be a writer for the high school newspaper. His buddy contacted us, and we had a discussion where we were able to share with him that the real story wasn't about Adam; rather, the real story was about the effect Adam had on everyone else. He penned an article entitled "The Adam Effect," and for our family it was the beginning of one of the greatest life-changing impacts we have ever experienced."

Duke had been so passionate about telling this story you could see the emotion expressed on his face and in his movements. Sue was batting clean-up and finished the story. "What Adam had taught us is that we *all* have an opportunity, every day, to have a positive impact on the people we encounter. We asked ourselves what we were doing so that we could inspire others and share joy, love, and happiness? It really had nothing to do with whether we had a disability or not. It had to do with who we were and what we represented. It had to do with our character. It allowed us to examine our thoughts, our words, and our actions, all of which define the character of who we really are."

Duke jumped back in. "Here's one story that defines more deeply the life lessons we learned from having Adam as our son. It includes several 'aha' moments during the time it took Adam to acquire the skill of walking. Adam's older brother successfully began walking at about ten and half months, which is average. Government studies show that 93.5 percent of children can successfully walk by thirteen months. Adam successfully learned to walk right before his second birthday, nearly *twenty-four* months. All kids born with Down syndrome have low muscle tone. It's one of the characteristics that affects their physical development, including hand/eye coordination, strength development, sight development, and speech. I say that not to worry you but to help you be prepared. We came to appreciate all of the support and therapy offered in our community to support Adam's development in all areas. We were able to access speech therapy, physical therapy, occupational therapy, and even music therapy as we navigated this path that was different from our firstborn's. All of that will be available to you once your child enters this world."

Sue needed to pull Duke back to the point of telling the story and jumped in.

"Back to Adam learning to walk. Both Duke and I had something in common at this point in our marriage. We had mastered being *impatient*. After all, we were doers—get-it-done kind of people, no-excuse-tolerated practitioners—and we both admired that neither of us had a hitch in our giddy-up. I'm just sayin', it took *forever* for Adam to learn to walk. During that time we were forced to be patient. His attempts were moving so slow that it was impossible to clearly pick a date on which we thought he would achieve walking successfully. So Adam taught us that there's great value practicing patience, in most every circumstance in life.

"The patience we were learning to employ waiting for Adam to walk began to have a positive effect on our interactions with everyone, including Adam's older brother, our parents, our siblings, our coworkers, our neighbors, and even people we met for the very first time. We noticed that this new patience made us better listeners, more compassionate people, and more encouraging to others. Think about the following statement: When we learn a lesson fast, we bypass the potential analysis, utilization, and understanding that lesson could positively impact our life with. We're too quick to move on, rendering the lesson near useless. The patience Adam's walking journey provided us with slowed us down so that we could learn a lesson for all the value it offered, rather than attempting to learn it fast. When it came to lesson-learning, the return on that patience investment was astronomical.

"Experiencing Adam learning to walk taught us never to judge another person. We learned that the only two people able to judge someone is the person someone sees in the mirror and God. Yet, previous to witnessing Adam's journey to walk, we were, in some cases, quick to judge others based on next to nothing. While we felt it was sad and unfair for people to judge Adam by the length of time it was taking him to learn to walk, we're so grateful that Adam's walking journey taught us not to judge others. Other people didn't have the same opportunity to learn what Adam was providing us with. We're better humans because of it."

Duke continued, "Adam's walking journey also provided both of us with an opportunity to talk about all of the things in life we had given up on. Although the range was wide, from figuring a certain career path just wasn't in our cards to never being able to ride a unicycle, we marveled at how Adam would fall, hurt himself, and get right back up and try again. It's so strange how *each of us* is born with the innate ability to never give up, proven by each of us who can walk. Just consider the number of times a child fails in an attempt to walk and is undeterred in the decision to try again. Witnessing Adam trying over and over made us ponder how we came to lose the drive necessary for success that we possessed as mere infants. While pondering, Sue and I became determined to assess all of the challenges we faced in life and determine which of them was important enough to keep pursuing. The first was our marriage. We recommitted to our vows and embraced once again that we would never give up on each other. We've attempted to utilize the 'never give up' attitude in every area of our life. Thanks for that, Adam."

Sue had more to share. "Another wonderful lesson Adam's journey of learning to walk provided us with was the power of encouragement. We would witness Adam trying so hard, and we felt compelled to encourage him in all that he did. We liberally encouraged him on a consistent basis. We realized that this also worked well with his older brother … and with each other … and with all of the people we knew. We had never really thought about it but concluded that there isn't *any* person that doesn't benefit from encouragement. In fact, as we began to focus on encouraging people every chance we had, we noticed people achieving more and experiencing more success with even the slightest amount of morale-boosting. We could clearly see the positive impact encouragement had on each other as we became each other's biggest cheerleader. Duke and I both agree that we never would have taken the time to fully learn and understand the role encouragement can play in other people's lives if we hadn't been along for the ride on Adam's journey of learning to walk. What an incredible world it could be if we all added the role of cheerleader to our daily life."

Amy had a question she was afraid to ask but really needed to know the answer to. She had a hard time summoning the courage but finally threw it out there: "Will our child look different? I mean, will people notice that they look different? Will other people stare, or be afraid, if they notice the difference? And how do you respond if they do?"

Sue immediately responded with a mother's compassion:

"Yes. People will most likely notice and in most cases it will create an opportunity for the two of you when it happens. It's strange,
anyone over the age of six may notice the ever-so-slight trademarks
of Down syndrome. For the most part, kids under seven are oblivi-
ous to things like height, weight, skin color, religion preference, language differences, hair, clothes, disabilities and more. Us adults miss
out on a valuable lesson of being nonjudgmental that is right in
front of us when observing children under seven. Most of the stares,
fears, and more that people have regarding all people with disabilities comes from two things.

"First is a lack of information and education, along with misin-
formation regarding people with disabilities. They just haven't any
clue about what to say or how to act when around someone with a
disability. The second comes from what I like to call 'kitchen table
discussion.' From an early age, children are all ears, like sponges, whenever they hear their parents, older siblings, and other adults talking
about any subject. Many times, things are said at the kitchen table,
or within the four walls of the home, enables some people to talk
about things outside of their normal character.

"While it's an opportunity to learn about love, acceptance, compassion, and friendship, there are homes where children begin the
development of bigotry, prejudice, and poor behavior. This is where
children begin their own character development as they navigate new
experiences created by elementary school. Once they hit middle school,
their peer group begins to have the most influence on their character development, and all the things that other parents shared with
that peer group gets sorted and filed in that child's brain, including
how to react or respond to a person they know having a 'disability.'

Duke took over the explanation. "Every opportunity that arises
when we notice someone curious, afraid to say something so they

won't make a mistake, or even attempting to treat our son differently than they would anyone else, we always jump on that opportunity to help that person understand what's similar about Adam and them. Adam likes chocolate ice cream, a good joke, music, and having fun just as much as you do…. and then we manage, and downplay, the differences between them. We attempt to transform their mind from concentrating on what's different to focusing on what's the same. We're nearly always successful with this strategy and have appreciated the positive impact it's had on Adam's life and the life of people who have given us the opportunity to teach. That lesson will serve them well into the future. An example is a local business owner that coached Adam on a Little League baseball team. He took what he had learned from the experience of coaching Adam and hired four adults with disabilities to work full-time for his company. We just see that as such a powerful byproduct of the Adam Effect. This is just another example of the many blessings we've enjoyed having a child with disabilities. All in all, it's been a completely positive life-changing experience for each of us in our family. And it can be for you too!"

It was difficult to tell, but it appeared that David and Amy were mesmerized by Duke and Sue's story. As they listened, they themselves felt encouraged, and, without consciously noticing, they were experiencing a sense of calm and a feeling of joy that their future was about to include all of these positive life lessons that few get to enjoy. They began to envision that they had been invited to a group they would eventually come to view as the Lucky Few.

Sue and Duke were both smiling. Knowing that there would be many more, they both believed that they had reached the goals they had set for themselves in this first meeting with Amy and David. Duke concluded the session. "In the end we realized how much Adam had changed—no, sorry, scratch that. We realized how much Adam had *improved* and *enhanced* our lives. And he still does, equally as much as our three other sons, who have benefitted from the lessons learned by having a brother with disabilities. Adam has had a similar impact on each of their lives with the same lessons we've had the privilege of learning. That's precisely why we can't imagine anyone who's given the chance not embracing the privilege of having a child with a disability. That's also why other like-minded people joined us in forming the club we mentioned when we first greeted you, the club we call Those Chosen for the Privilege. Thus, we'd like to offer you the opportunity to embrace **The Gift of Being Chosen for the Privilege**. We hope that you'll not only embrace this gift but be willing to share it with all that you encounter from this day forward."

With a polite knock on the door, Adam waited to be invited into the Room of Caring, and it was David and Amy that waved for him to enter. This was turning into a day all of them would never forget.

THE GIFT OF MODELING

t turned out to be a birthday gift that he was giving to himself. Thirty was a significant number of years, and Dennis figured he was ready for a significant step of some kind in his life. He just wasn't sure what that step should look like. Life was good. He'd done well in school, scored a great job with a contemporary corporation that was moving forward, was still deeply in love with his wife of five years, and was enjoying the fatherhood experience with his three-year-old daughter and one-year-old son.

Dennis felt he owed the joy he experienced in life to one word, and that word was *discipline*. It had been at the foundation of all he had achieved so far, and he credited his parents with forging the word into a tool he could utilize in every area of his life. Dennis chuckled as memories came to mind of his parents drilling their favorite quote into his mind as a parenting method to combat the pursuit of instant gratification that drove the lives of people in today's internet society. His parents' favorite quote emanated from our sixteenth president, Abraham Lincoln. They utilized it with Dennis every chance they could until it became second nature for him to embrace its wisdom: "Discipline is choosing between what you want *now* and what you want *most.*" Dennis had grown up with a dream of making a difference in the world and felt that, at the age of thirty, he was moving in the right direction but needed significant help developing a long-term strategy that could have a lasting impact accomplishing what he wanted most.

Hitting any significant number of birthdays that end with either a zero or a five typically causes a person to look backwards and reflect. Dennis had been reflecting over the past week and had really embraced the gratitude he felt for being given the gift of such a wonderful life. Along with the lesson of discipline and the role it played in his life, his parents had raised him emphasizing the positive power of living a selfless life and the regret that typically envelops living a selfish life. In his thirty years, he had witnessed enough examples of both to commit to wanting to teach his own children this powerful lesson, along with Lincoln's quote regarding discipline that his parents had so lovingly taught him. It was this particular reflection that had led him to the Answer Discovery that day at lunchtime. He had heard enough about the Answer Discovery to know that people with problems went there and, through some process, found answers.

Dennis' wife originally had planned on meeting him for a special lunch, but he had explained that he was feeling called in some strange way to visit the unique building that could help him answer the question that had popped up in the front of his mind recently: *What next?*

He loved his wife so much. When he had told her what he wanted to do at lunchtime on his birthday, she shifted gears and made him his favorite breakfast: avocado toast with a soft-boiled egg on top. What a wonderful way to begin the day. She also had given him a unique gift that morning that first made him laugh and then made him cry, being so filled with joy. Her gift was a wooden picture frame with two words hand-carved across the top: FOREVER YOUNG.

This made him laugh, as he was only celebrating his thirtieth birthday, and then he began to cry when he looked at what she had placed inside the frame. It was a picture of them on their wedding day, next to the lyrics from the Rod Stewart song "Forever Young." She had begun to play the song as he was opening the gift. Dennis had never really paid close attention to the lyrics before. As he listened to the song while reading the lyrics, he glanced up at his wife and had a beautiful moment of clarity as to just how deep his love was for her, and her love for him. The lyrics were a perfect way of expressing their love for each other. She was completely supportive of how he would spend his lunchtime that day and very eager to hear what would transpire at the fabled Answer Discovery.

A few hours later, Dennis had parked, inhaled a deep breath of courage, and headed for the door of the uniquely named building. He felt an unexplained attraction to the place and entered with a quiet confidence that was free of any ego. When he had taken no more than three steps inside, the words, HAPPY BIRTHDAY, DENNIS. SO GLAD THAT YOU CHOSE TO BE HERE TODAY, were communicated to him. He was neither alarmed nor concerned about this strange occurrence. "It just seemed so natural," he would later recall.

"I hope it's okay that I came," Dennis responded.

IT APPEARS TO BE PART OF YOUR DESTINY. KNOWING THAT YOUR FAMILY REGULARLY ATTENDS CHURCH ON SUNDAY MORNING, IT'S REQUESTED THAT YOU VISIT A GENTLEMAN NAMED OTIS THIS COMING SUNDAY AFTERNOON AT 2:30. HE'LL BE WAITING FOR YOU AT THE GREAT TRAVERSE SWEETS COMPANY, LOCATED ON THE CORNER OF WALLOON AND GLEN ARBOR AVENUES. YOU'LL EASILY IDENTIFY HIM, AND YOU SHOULD BLOCK ABOUT TWO HOURS OF TIME TO SHARE WITH OTIS. IT'S ACKNOWLEDGED THAT SUNDAY IS NORMALLY DEVOTED TO YOUR FAMILY, BUT THIS EXCEPTION WILL GREATLY BENEFIT ALL OF YOU IN THE LONG RUN.

"Thank you," Dennis replied. "I'll be there Sunday afternoon. I'm really excited!" Dennis had anticipated receiving an answer that day but felt confident that a plan had been formulated that would help him move forward in all the different areas of his life.

• • •

Sunday arrived, and shortly after the church service his family had attended, he realized how grateful he was that he was meeting Otis on a Sunday afternoon. He had really opened his mind while listening to the sermon that day. The sermon was based on the words from Jeremiah 29:11: For I know the plans I have for you. Plans to prosper you and not to harm you. Plans to give you hope and a future. Coincidence? Dennis wasn't sure, but he couldn't imagine a more perfect message to begin his day with.

Upon arriving at the Great Traverse Sweets Company, Dennis parked and once again took in a deep breath of courage, then exhaled, letting the excitement and enthusiasm build up within him. He wondered if his life would change much because of this meeting. He was about to realize that that was quite simply a complete understatement.

Dennis entered the building and looked around. He spotted Otis right away, as there was a small tent sign on his table that read Welcome Dennis. Two people from different areas of the store shouted, "Afternoon, Otis!" The man at the table waved a friendly "hello" with his arm as he engaged in a lively conversation with a woman. Otis was a big man who looked to be about sixty years old. When they had appeared to have completed the conversation, the woman smiled, thanked him, and walked toward the exit door. Dennis paused for a second and then approached Otis.

"It is a warm welcome I offer you today, Dennis," Otis said as he watched Dennis approaching. Then he stood up and extended his right hand to offer a warm handshake that continued with Otis placing his left hand on the side of Dennis's forearm to complete the traditional greeting.

Dennis responded, "It's so kind of you to meet with me today. While I'm not sure what to expect, I'm excited to listen to what you have to say to me."

"How's it going, Otis?" someone else offered from about twelve feet away. Otis glanced in the direction that the voice came from.

"Fine. I'm just about to get started with this young man. How's your wife's therapy and recovery coming along?"

"Super, thanks to your help preparing her before surgery for a stellar and fast path back to greatness."

"Please share with her that I'm very proud of her dedication to full recovery. I'm also proud of you for serving her so well during her surgery and recovery. The two of you continue to make a great team and a positive example for all of us to follow. Thanks for that, Jake!"

Jake finished by saying, "It brings us great joy to hear those words from you, Otis. I'll pass them along to my wife."

Otis smiled warmly at the man that sat across from him. "Are you ready, Dennis?" Dennis gently nodded in the affirmative.

Otis began, "You find yourself in a wonderful position in life. You have great balance in the areas that matter most, and you have a desire to seek what may be beyond. That alone creates a strong foundation from which to advance. I'm going to add a solid block to your foundation today. This block will help you grow into your destiny. During that growth, much will be given to you, and because of that much will be expected of you. The expectations are set so that the seeds that will be planted within you germinate, sprout, and then produce. Nothing is sadder than great potential going to waste, and so you'll utilize the block I mentioned to create your own measuring system that measures yourself against yourself. Are you with me so far?"

Otis paused to make sure Dennis was in tune with his communication style. It always helped to assess this early on and attempt to determine what type of learner was sitting across the table from him. In fact, Otis had spent years fine-tuning his discussions to include the widest range of learners, and he always had some visual aids available to supplement his explanations if needed. Dennis had a warm smile on his face, and his eyes indicated that he was paying close attention and was ready to hang on every word coming out of Otis's mouth.

Otis smiled, because it had taken him a long time to become the man he was today. He knew that at some point he would reveal to Dennis how he had experienced drug addiction, homelessness, and an inability to hold a job at points in his life. He'd also share how a man named Jason had saved him from committing suicide as he taught Otis many of the things Otis would be sharing today. Just not yet. First, he needed to frame it right.

"The block being added to your life's foundation today is modeling. Before your subconscious goes down the path of associating this with wearing new fashions and walking down a runway, let me clarify: it doesn't! The modeling I'm talking about is based on the premise that there isn't any challenge that occurs in any of our lives that hasn't been successfully solved and mastered by someone else before us. Finding one or more individuals that have solved and mastered a challenge we find ourselves facing is key. I say both solved *and* mastered to make note that many people temporarily solve a challenge but fall victim to the same challenge recurring as time goes by.

"An example of that is losing weight. Many have lost weight (i.e., solved the challenge) but gained the weight back over time (i.e., failed to master the challenge). In a search for an individual who has both solved and mastered the weight-loss challenge, we would want to seek out someone who both lost the desired amount of weight, and then maintained the goal weight consistently over a five-year period.

Five years seems an appropriate amount of time for weight loss and maybe something like smoking. Longer periods of time to show mastery might be more appropriate for challenges like alcohol, drug, or a gambling addiction. There are many good programs out there available to help people with those types of challenges, with the mastery goal being 'until death do we part.' Individuals who have a long-term track record of mastery with those challenges are normally the ones deeply involved in the program, helping newcomers with hope, respect, appreciation for what they're facing, and encouragement.

"Now, back to how modeling will have an important impact on who you turn out to be. Modeling works in every area of our life. Let me use myself as an example. I was able to totally screw up my life by the time I turned twenty. By that age I had mastered the utilization of modeling. The problem turned out to be that my choice of whom to model was seriously flawed. When I first arrived at college, I saw people partying and having fun. It looked like something I would enjoy, and so I modeled their behavior until I ended up addicted to cocaine. Nothing else in life mattered more than the next score … and it was *expensive*.

"By the middle of my sophomore year, I had dropped out of school. I moved out of the dorm and into a dump. I fell behind on rent, and the landlord provided me with a free ride to the city limits with a box of what few belongings I had left, including a battered old tent. I lived in that tent, deep in the woods on state land, where no one would bother me. I worked jobs just long enough to feed my drug addiction. One day while I was hitchhiking, a man named Jason stopped to offer a ride. I didn't realize he was a counselor at a drug rehab center until we pulled up to where he worked. The hardest decision I have ever made in my life was to allow Jason to walk me through the front door. But it was the beginning of a new beginning.

"Once I moved several years past the dark period in my life with

Jason's help, I wanted to make positive modeling my own. I wanted to create something that I could use effectively as evidence of validity in my own life and then be able to teach it to others. I was having a face-to-face talk with the man in the mirror. It was kind of a strange day where my brain's gears were turning so fast, I swear I could smell burnt rubber. Married at the time, I wondered what the best husband in the world looked like. We had kids by then, and I asked myself what the best father in the world looked like. With both of my parents still alive at the time, I was curious as to what the best son in the world would be doing on a day like today.

"This thought process quickly began to morph into something huge. I started wondering about the best neighbor, the best cousin, the best uncle, the best boss, the best coworker, the best student, the best educator, the best mentor, the best community member, the best member of the state and country, and just for fun I threw in the very best person in the world. What did they all look like, and even more importantly, *why* would someone come to that conclusion? What did they have in common? What did they do differently, and was the difference huge or subtle? Was it a conglomeration of things they did a little bit better than others, or was it one particular thing they did so well that it propelled them ahead of everyone else? Now you know why I thought I smelled burnt rubber."

Dennis laughed and found himself sitting on the edge of his seat, waiting for Otis to continue. Otis paused, took a sip of water, and then continued.

"I had this insatiable desire to pursue this line of thinking, and so I gave myself the task of developing a system and skill set that would help me accomplish framing what the best person would look like in all of these instances. During the process I developed a new set of listening skills that allowed me to pick up on conversations I heard between people I know where someone was saying something nice about someone else. I would wait for an appropriate opening and then engage the person who had said the nice things with a statement and then a question, like:

"'Wow, you're saying some really nice things about someone, and you really seem to appreciate them. How did that come to be?' The answers I heard were very broad, and ranged from, 'They've just always been kind to me,' to, 'They saved my life.' I developed some simple follow-up statements and questions that allowed me to dive deeper into why this person meant so much to them. Sometimes it was as simple as asking them to tell me more. My abilities to gain knowledge from these interactions grew, and one day I realized that I had learned a tremendous amount about *what meant the most to people in their relationships with others.*

"I spent time interacting with the people whom others so admired and developed a list of qualities that set people apart from, and ahead of, others in every category I had originally listed: husband, father, son, coworker, etc. Then I set about finding people I already knew who possessed those qualities and began to model their behavior and patterns. I supplemented all of this with books about people who had stood out positively in our society, finding at least one thing that these people, whether historical or current, were doing right, and then implemented it into my own daily behavior. All part of modeling.

"The most exciting part was taking thought processes and behavior that I admired from a large group of individuals and packaging them into who I wanted to be, selecting the best of everyone to become the very best version of myself. The challenge now became, 'How do I restructure my life so that, in every area, I'm making consistent progress on becoming the best husband, father, son, coworker, and on and on?' Others I saw successfully improving in the important areas of their life seemed to have mastered what I can best describe as being in the present moment. And so I modeled that skill.

"When I was with my wife, my mind would be engaged in everything I was saying and doing, attempting to say and do, based on what the best husband in the world would. Was I perfect right from the get-go? No. But I recognized positive momentum as my relationship with my wife improved steadily to the point that, one day, she shared with me that she had noticed a difference in me and how happy she was to be married to me. Then she proclaimed me to be the best husband in the world. Modeling had worked!

"Let's go back to the beginning. When I set out to be the best husband in the world, was I attempting to have some worldwide organization proclaim that I was? No. There was really only one person that I wanted to claim me as the best husband in the world. That was my wife. And that also doesn't mean that, once accomplished, the goal had lost its significance. The people I most admired, whom I had modeled my husband role after, had been that way for years, always improving and growing in that role.

"While successful in the moment, I realized that I could continue to utilize modeling to grow and deepen my role as a husband until death do us part. One side effect of this process is that I came to see my wife as the best wife in the world. The more I did for her, the more she did for me. Later in life I would recognize this as the power of reciprocity. I've enjoyed what I can only describe as the best marriage in the world ever since.

"The same thing happened with parenting. Both my wife and I were befuddled when we had our first child and realized they didn't come with a complete set of instructions. I know I'm a man, but I'm a man who's willing to ask for directions when I'm lost."

Dennis busted a gut at that statement. As he attempted to regain control of his concentration, Dennis raised his hand. "Dennis... When

I'm on a roll, I speak at an average rate of 160 words per minute, with gusts up to 200, but you don't need to raise your hand to interrupt me," Otis said. "What do you want to ask?"

"Well, I'm not quite sure that I understand why you thought you had to be the best at everything."

"Good thought. Imagine an unmarried individual who wants to find a spouse. They post on a dating site that they consider themselves average … Let's say a grade of 'C.' They acknowledge that a 'B' is better and an 'A' is best, but getting to 'A,' or even a 'B,' would take a lot of hard work and dedication. They have other interests in life, and while they desire a relationship that would lead to marriage, they're concerned about what they'd have to give up to be a 'B' or an 'A.' So they're looking for someone who will accept them as they are, someone who's at peace with mediocrity. Compare that with another person posting on that same dating site who says his primary goal is to be the best husband in the world someday. He admits to not being perfect and that he makes mistakes, but he indicates that he's constantly striving to learn ways that would make his future spouse happy and that he has a desire to always be striving to be the best until death do us part. Now, could you imagine me attempting to be anything less than the best in my wife's eyes? This reminds me of one of my favorite sayings: 'Mediocrity: any time we settle for less than who we really are and who we were meant to be.' I just can't imagine having one of my foundational blocks of life saying 'mediocre' on it. On the other hand, I understand what it can mean to have a foundational block that says, 'Striving to always be the best me.' Are we on the same page?"

Dennis nodded his head and said, "Yes. I get it. Thank you."

"Awesome. Now back to striving to be the best father. Modeling was critical in the parenting style my wife and I developed. While we read a lot of books and articles on parenting—and they helped a ton—we became expert observers of what other parents were doing whenever we encountered them. Maybe we were at a store, a restaurant, preschool, play groups, church, family gatherings, a park—we observed what other parents were doing. It never mattered where we were; we were all over them like sprinkles on a birthday cake. We also became expert observers of children's television, books, stories, toys, and my personal favorite: any tools that helped infants and children stop crying and start sleeping."

Again, Dennis began to laugh as his mind wandered for a moment to the different tools that he and his wife had come to depend on to alleviate crying and encourage sleeping. Those occurrences were in the process of becoming cherished memories. Dennis was really becoming drawn to Otis. Admittedly, he was kind of quirky, but Dennis was starting to realize that he would remember this day for the rest of his life.

Meanwhile, Otis stood up and motioned for Dennis to do the same. Otis then said, "Deep breath in through the nose, out through the mouth using a one-two-three count. Inhale deeply for a one count, then take three times as long to exhale. Well done. Let's sit back down and pick up where I left off."

Otis knew that every so often he needed to break up the intensity of what he was teaching with something like the quick breathing exercise. It allowed both of them to hit the refresh button and get back to the present with renewed energy. Dennis smiled as he sat back down and was thankful for the brief interruption as he placed his mind and his attention back on what Otis was saying.

"It's important to note that while we were observing other parents, we never judged. We had learned early on that we could never know enough about someone else's life to pass judgment on them. Instead, we became hyper-focused on cause and effect, or 'outcomes measurement,' as we matured in our learning. We learned the importance of consequences, both good and bad, and tying them to specific behavior. As we advanced further, we had what we can only refer to as an epiphany when we finally understood the power of the 'why' and the impact it could have. We observed that the children of people getting the desired results from their parenting appeared to be able to explain the 'why' of the expectations their parents had of them.

"And I'm not just talking about teen and young adult children. I'm talking about kids as young as three. My wife would tell you that just the threat of, 'Do you want me to have your father explain *why* what you're about to do, which you know is wrong, is a bad thing for you to do when he gets home?' was enough to prevent undesired action and behavior on our children's part. We laugh about it now but stand behind how powerful the 'why' has been in our life. It was at this point that I began to notice people utilizing this 'why theory' at work, in nonprofits whose boards I served on, and in leadership books I read. It turns out that all people really appreciate knowing the 'why' behind every part of their lives.

'Companies and organizations with the very best cultures are made up of people at every level that can explain *why* they do what they do. They have purpose, and they embrace it with an understanding that every member of the team plays an integral role in accomplishing the 'why' in what they do.

"This all ties back to the word *best*, and why we could all strive to be the best at what we do, in every important area of our life, each and every day. People who we can model are out there. They may be in an autobiography of a historical person. They may attend the church we belong to. They may be our neighbor, coworker, friend, acquaintance, relative, someone we meet through a business interaction, or someone that we've noticed and admired for something they've achieved in some specific area of life. Seek out people you admire and ask them questions. When someone shows admiration, respect, and interest in an individual, that individual is willing to share what has helped them become a person worth modeling.

"Dennis, you have an incredible path laid out for you to follow. Master modeling, and you will discover all that you are capable of being in every area of life that's important to you. As you are in the process of mastering the art of modeling and discovering a life beyond awesome, always take time to reflect on the 'why.'"

Dennis interrupted Otis. "I believe I just discovered the 'why.' All of this I will do in hopes that one day I will be someone's Otis, sharing all I have learned through modeling and passing those lessons on to them in the hope they will pay it forward someday. It sounds like we're nearing the end of our discussion, but before I depart, I'd like to ask *you* a few questions based on things that I've observed over the last two hours of meeting with you. Questions like: Why did ten other people stand and take a deep breath, in through the nose and out through the mouth, at the same time you and I did? And why did every person who picked up one of the cards you placed on the table next to us seem to tear it in half, write something on each half, and then place one in your bag and one in the bag labeled with my name on it? And why didn't I think to take notes the entire time I've been here?"

Otis smiled warmly as he looked deep into Dennis's eyes. In those eyes he saw the hope of the world. He could feel it. This brought him great joy. Then Otis finally spoke in a soft, well-seasoned voice. "Dennis, those are wonderful questions. Every one of those ten people who stood when we stood have sat in the chair you now occupy. They come here on days like today and share with each other the progress they've made utilizing modeling in the important areas of their life. Standing with us and repeating the quick breathing exercise brings great memories of the past and great hope for the future. They tore the card in half so that the message of hope and encouragement they wrote to you relates to the message they wrote to me. One year from now, you and I will meet again, match the notes based on how they were torn, and discuss the messages that were sent to both of us and how they relate. Finally, the reason you didn't take notes is because, like with all the people I meet with, I have an outline to give you that includes everything I shared today. It can be a powerful tool as you pursue modeling and a life beyond awesome. Embrace and enjoy **The Gift of Modeling.** Your life is about to soar."

THE GIFT OF MENTORING

Martha loved her job, and she was good at it. Her board of directors had just told her so, along with providing an increase in pay and a substantial bonus. She had been selected to lead the local chamber of commerce as its president just shy of three years ago and had accomplished a lot. That included inspiring the people she worked with to achieve more than they thought they could and introducing many new programs designed to help the membership, along with a unique initiative that brought businesses and the greater community together as one.

As she paused for a moment to enjoy the appreciation that had been bestowed upon her, she opened her mind up to all of the good that was still possible to achieve moving forward. She knew that she was surrounded on all sides by untapped resources, but she couldn't figure out how to identify, and then pursue, the opportunities those untapped resources presented. She had heard stories—many from people she admired and had a personal relationship with—about the Answer Discovery, and after having just been graced with the unanimous support of her board, she felt it was time for her own personal visit to this slightly mysterious yet welcoming building.

While still riding the tidal wave of joy she had received from her board, Martha entered the Answer Discovery. She noted that any-time she entered into an experience filled with joy, it always seemed to elevate the results on the other end, and right now she was ultra-excited to walk into the most unique and welcoming space she had ever experienced. As Martha entered, she noticed that she felt similar to when she was comfortable at home, enjoying time free from the worries that presented themselves each day. She wasn't confused or sur-prised when she became aware that she was being communicated to.

It's so nice to welcome you here today, Martha. Congratu-lations on your wonderful review this morning. Your future will consistently improve, as will the lives of all the people you will impact. Your time here will be short, as there is a man named Antonio who awaits your arrival at the coffee and bak-ery shop called Inspired by Love, which is on the opposite side of the block from where you now stand. Antonio is an older gentleman, and you will see his charcoal-colored fedora hat sitting on the table he is reserving for you. He will be shar-ing a thought process that will help you lead others to the very top of where they would like to be. Today will be a day you will remember for the rest of your life as you reflect on all the things you have yet to accomplish. Embrace and enjoy this day. Thank you for visiting the Answer Discovery.

Martha, realizing that this part of the experience was about to end, took one last look around and committed all she saw to her memory file. This was one memory she wanted to hold onto forever. After she anchored the memory, she was out the door. It was a beautiful day. She knew right where she was going, as the Inspired by Love Cof-fee and Bakery Shoppe was a chamber member, and she decided to walk around the block. She was excited to meet Antonio and won-dered what this gentleman had to share with her.

All that had really been communicated by the Answer Discovery is that it would play a significant role in her life. She decided the beautiful day could wait as she picked up her pace, now only a hundred yards away from the place she had been led to. It would be her second visit there that day, as it was her routine to utilize their drive-thru for her first cup of coffee each day. She always felt good about supporting a chamber member.

* * *

As Martha walked in front of the huge floor-to-ceiling windows that fronted the coffee and bakery shop, she glanced inside and saw an elderly man with the kindest face she had ever seen. She glanced at the table he was seated at, and, sure enough, there was the charcoal-colored fedora hat with a colorful feather pin fastened to its side. Martha had just turned thirty-two, and the hat brought back fond memories of her grandfather, who had a hat just like it.

Martha had just entered the shop when she heard, "Martha. Welcome back for round two. The usual?" It was the voice of the owner, Gigi, from behind the counter. "That would be awesome," Martha replied with a smile. She turned her attention to the table with the hat. Antonio was beginning to stand and extend his hand for a warm handshake when he said, "Welcome, Martha. This is such a special day for me. Thank you for being the one to make it special. I'm Antonio."

Martha was thankful that a person's mind can work so much faster than the pace of speech. She was processing what Antonio had just said about it being a special day for *him* when she replied, "It is *I* who should be doing the thanking, but, judging from the smile on both of our faces, it appears that it is intended to be a special day for the both of us."

Just then Gigi set down Martha's second coffee of the day in front of her and refilled a bright yellow mug with a smiley face on it in front of Antonio with hot water, setting a fresh tea bag down beside his mug. Indicating Antonio had already prepaid for everything they would consume that day, Gigi said, "Compliments of my mentor, Antonio." To which Antonio replied, "Lovingly prepared by my mentor, Gigi." The smiles and the upbeat attitudes were contagious. Martha realized that this moment in time was special. She would embrace this moment.

"May I ask you a question?" Antonio began.

"Sure," replied Martha.

"Do you recall the two of us ever meeting before today?"

"Not that I remember, and I feel like I would remember a face filled with such hope and kindness, which is what I see before me now."

"Thanks for the kind words. I like you already. I don't ever remember us meeting either, but I'm glad we're meeting today. Here's another question: Would you be willing to believe that when you change the way you look at things, the things you look at change?"

Martha answered, "Wow, that's deep. But, sure. Yes, I can believe that statement. It reminds me of the definition of a paradigm shift."

"Exactly!" Antonio said with enthusiasm.

"I've been asked to share with you today the knowledge I've acquired regarding a single word. I hope to change the way you look at that word and what it can mean. That word has had the greatest impact on both my personal and professional life. Through the years I've developed a unique perspective regarding the word. That word is 'mentoring,' and often it's called by another name. Some substitute names might be 'parenting,' 'guiding,' 'informing,' 'teaching,' 'caring for,' 'loving,' 'providing,' 'enlightening,' and many more. I hope you're not in a hurry today. For months I have been preparing for this day, and I'd like it to last long enough for the joy of it to linger forever in my mind. Having said that, here's the story of what mentoring has meant for me.

"When I was thirty-seven years old, I was on top of my game. Everything was going right in both my professional and my personal life. It was hard to imagine a better life, but that's the same thing I had been saying for the previous fifteen years, since I had graduated from college. Loving analysis, I sat down and reflected on all the things that had contributed to getting me to where I was. After a couple of hours of searching my memory bank, I realized something that had never occurred to me before. During every step of my life, there had been a specific person that had either taken me under their wing, given me direction, helped me with a challenge, prevented me from making a major blunder, introduced me to a different thought process, connected me to another person, or educated me. I really owed my life to people that had mentored me.

"This pause for reflection created an overwhelming feeling of *gratitude*. The overwhelming feeling of gratitude created a desire to study and more clearly understand what this gratitude was founded on. That led me to pursue the definition, and a deep understanding, of the word *mentoring*. The more I studied mentoring, the more I realized that it was one of the most important parts of every area of my life and that there would be great value in becoming an expert in it. So I set about to become a mentoring expert, which is why you and I are sitting at this table today.

"As I acquired information and knowledge regarding mentoring, I came to the conclusion that mentoring could be divided into four unique and different types. The four types are:

1. Being Mentored by Others

2. Self-Mentoring

3. Mentoring Others

4. Group Mentoring

"I set about to define each area and the impact it could have on a person's life.

"Being Mentored by Others begins at birth. Our parents are the primary mentors. They are loaded with love for us, and the primary driver of their mentoring is *hope* for our future. Everything they do for us is designed with *our* best interests in their heart. It's truly amazing when you consider all the different areas of life they attempt to cover in order to prepare us for the day they release us on our own to the greater world. It occurred to me that they have support and help from others along the way, possibly including grandparents, siblings, daycare workers, preschool teachers, neighbors, and fellow church members if they regularly attend. Then the support they receive moves into a new phase, with K–12 teachers and staff representing a large part of their children's available attention span each day.

"As we're growing up, we don't recognize this as mentoring, and we take it for granted that our parents and others are just fulfilling the roles they've taken on. Thinking this through, I became obsessed with the idea that my wife and I could teach our three children, all under the age of ten at the time, to develop the perspective that they could be *grateful* for everything they had learned that day because of the effort someone had made to improve their knowledge and, thus, their life. Then they would appreciate the efforts other people made on their behalf and, crucially, *have a desire to show them that they appreciated that someone cared that much about them.* This might translate into working and studying harder and always doing their best, which could lead to grade improvement.

"For our children, it led to consistently performing the chores they had been entrusted with, understanding how much better the family life as a whole was when they did their part. When we began to see positive results with our children, my wife and I began developing ways for *ourselves* to create openings for being mentored by others. I feel one of the most powerful tools we developed, often overlooked, is the power of curiosity—something both my wife and I were loaded with. We ended up developing questions that kick-started most of the relationships we developed with people willing to mentor us.

"We were constantly refining the questions to obtain the desired results. For example, instead of asking someone a poorly worded question such as, 'How in the world have you been able to make so much money?' we would get incredible results asking, 'If there were one thing you could attribute all your success to, what would it be?' As we learned, we shared the knowledge we were acquiring with our children, so that by the time they finished high school and headed to college, they were well prepared to seek out mentors and convince them that the time spent mentoring would not be wasted but rather would result in benefits for everyone.

"While these college mentors may have realized that our kids weren't going to be first in their class, they sensed that they had a unique perspective on obtaining success in both their professional and personal lives. They carried that same acquisition of mentors into adult life, experiencing rapid advancement and success in their professional careers and consistent joy and happiness in their personal lives. Their strong curiosity and willingness to admit they have areas in their lives they want to learn more about, as well as the respect they have for anyone who knows more about something than they do, has been the foundation of embracing being mentored by others.

"The second type of mentoring turns out to be most people's favorite. I call it Self-Mentoring, because the person pursuing it has complete control over its level of success. It's really driven by your own personal desire to satisfy your curiosity. Anytime you grow your level of curiosity, you drive forward your desire to self-mentor, and self-mentoring is really another term for 'research.' We mentor ourselves each time we perform research or take advantage of a unique opportunity to grow ourselves through videos, podcasts, articles, books, and information available on the internet. We mentor ourselves when we ask questions seeking a deeper understanding about something.

"Self-mentoring is an option if you want to lose weight, if you want to purchase a vehicle, if you want to know more about a medical diagnosis you just received, if you want to plant a garden, if you want to improve your proficiency with your occupation, if you want to travel, if you want to create a personal budget, if you want to deepen relationships, if you want to start a family, if you have a child with disabilities, if you want to promote peace, if you want to grow as a person, and more. I could go on for hours.

"The truth is, in today's world there isn't anything limiting you about any subject. The ability to self-mentor is yours for the taking. Given that we all learn differently, once you master the most efficient way of educating *yourself*, the world is your oyster (which is old-guy talk for *can you even believe how easy it is to grow our mind and knowledge?*). That's why mastery of self-mentoring is such an important part of mentoring as a whole.

"The key to self-mentoring is determining the level of curiosity you have regarding something and being open to the different ways you can satisfy that curiosity. When I attempt to teach someone the art of self-mentoring, my goal is to allow them to view everyday occurrences from a new perspective that allows for them to see life lessons in a place they had missed before. I'm going to give you some strange examples that never seem to be on other people's radar screen but that have played prominent roles in my own self-mentoring.

"I've lost track of the number of times I've watched the movie *It's a Wonderful Life*. The first time I watched it, I liked it, but it didn't provide anything other than me enjoying a nice story. The second time I watched it, I noticed a plaque in the background of a scene in the main character's office under his father's picture. I couldn't read it all at first, but my curiosity got the better of me, and I backed it up and paused until it was clearly visible enough to read it. I was amazed at what I saw, and the funny thing was, the words were never spoken by anyone in the movie. It was just a random background piece that someone must have thought helped define the father's character ... *and it did.* The plaque read:

ALL YOU CAN TAKE WITH YOU
IS THAT WHICH YOU'VE GIVEN AWAY

"I spent hours thinking about that quote and how it could have a positive impact on my life. I came up with several ways that I began to institute until they became a natural part of my personal 'Life's Principles Collection.' All because of a plaque hidden in the background of a classic movie scene. Do you see how that's a form of self-mentoring?"

Martha replied, "I do. I clearly do."

Antonio continued, "The second self-mentoring lesson from that same movie was when the angel character tells the main character, 'You've been given a great gift. A chance to see what the world would be like without you.' It may have been the third or fourth time I was watching the movie, and that quote hit me like a ton of bricks (which is old-guy talk for 'really hard'). Soon after, I devoted an entire Saturday analyzing what the world would be like had *I* never been born. I knew enough not to be critical of my life thus far, and I swayed my mind to focus more on missed opportunities where I could have made a difference for others in the past. I treated this exercise like a 'Life Wake-Up Call' and set about training myself to be more of a noticer. By 'noticer,' I mean always looking for opportunities and pausing long enough to make a difference. It was a pivotal point in my life regarding my understanding of how self-mentoring could be a powerful force in the shaping of my character and attainment of my goals."

Antonio could clearly see that Martha was paying close attention by the affirmative nodding of her head. He took another long sip of his tea.

"The third type of mentoring comes with a foundation of humility, hope, and joy. Mentoring Others is best and at its highest level when it's considered a privilege. It's like being given a reward before you even deliver it. The reward is based on all the people that have helped you in your life. Now you're being given the opportunity to pay it forward. Mentoring others typically begins without us ever being aware that it's happening.

"It might start at home when you help a younger sibling learn to walk or ride a bike or learn a game. It may have its origin during an athletic practice or game when you notice someone struggling with something you've already learned and you attempt to help them improve. It may occur when you work on a school project as part of team. Later it may be a classmate that asks for help in a subject that you can explain really well. As you begin your work life, it may be utilizing your area of expertise to help others focused on a different area of the business. It may also be listening to a friend and offering compassion and loving care.

"When I was attempting to learn more about this particular area of mentoring, I became aware that the people I noticed that were most consistently happy, and living what appeared to be a wonderful life, were the people that I admired the most. As I studied them more closely, I saw a consistency possessed by each of them. That consistency helped me come to the conclusion that the source of their daily joy was derived from helping others. In my mind, 'helping others' is just a synonym for 'mentoring.'

"Further, I realized that random acts of kindness are also a form of mentoring others. Science has shown that when anyone *performs* a random act of kindness, their body releases a dose of serotonin. Serotonin is a chemical we all have the ability to produce naturally that causes us to experience a sensation of joy and happiness. Studies also show that the person *receiving* the random act of kindness also experiences a release of serotonin. Even more incredible is that any person *witnessing* this random act of kindness has a natural release of serotonin. That's a win-win-win scenario. Is there anything better than a win-win-win?"

Martha had been listening so intently to everything Antonio was sharing that the question caught her off guard, and she wasn't sure if Antonio actually wanted her to answer it. She suddenly found herself blurting out, "No. Nope. That's pretty much the most desired outcome of any situation."

Antonio had used the question to create a pause, which allowed him to take another long sip of tea. He told Martha, "Sometimes I talk so much without a break that my mouth gets dry and my tongue gets stuck when I attempt to say certain words so, even though it was a rhetorical question, I asked that last question in order to give myself a chance to wet my whistle (which is old-guy talk for hydrating my mouth and vocal chords)."

Martha was becoming endeared to Antonio just by listening to the flow of how he spoke. She was happy to be sitting across from him. She also realized she had already learned a significant amount about something she had thought she understood. She was realizing that mentoring could be thought of so much deeper and that the rewards it offered were so much more significant than she had ever dreamed.

Antonio continued, "As I continued studying mentoring, I realized that the people I most admired at work spent a majority of their time helping other people at work be successful. I realized that the husbands I admired most spent a majority of their time helping their wives be successful. I realized that the fathers I most admired spent the majority of their time helping their children learn and grow. The community members I most admired spent a majority of their time helping other people. All of this related to a higher level of love that many people never get to experience. I had come to understand that 'mentoring' and 'helping other people' were interchangeable terms. I concluded that the combination of allowing people to mentor us and us mentoring other people was the solution to moving the world in a positive direction. These two types of mentoring both utilize self-mentoring and group mentoring as fuel to spread themselves far and wide. A win for individuals. A win for teams. A win for families. A win for communities. A win for countries. A win for the world. That's a lot of wins. The proper use of mentoring can improve people, improve work cultures, improve families, improve communities, improve countries, and change the world. The key to all of this is getting people to accept the power of mentoring and creating a desire for them to pursue the positive impact it can have for them. They need to believe that the results of embracing mentoring will bring them more joy, happiness, love, appreciation, and respect. As humans we crave all of these every day of our lives."

Martha quickly interjected the question, "So, Antonio, how would someone go about getting everyone to buy in to your mentoring theory?"

"Have I not convinced *you* that mentoring has the power to change the world?"

"Yeah, sure, I believe. But how do we get others to believe?"

Antonio offered another "old-guy talk" response when he said, "How do you eat an entire elephant? One bite at a time."

Then Martha asked, "Do you have any suggestions on where to begin? And, oh yeah, you haven't said anything about the fourth type of mentoring. Wasn't it Group Mentoring?"

"That's right, it's a concept I developed over the years that can turbo charge the foundation of the mentoring thought process. Let's start in the workplace. Teams are created based on what each individual member of the team can contribute to the team as a whole. It wouldn't make sense to have two members on a team that have mirror-image skill sets with similar levels of experience in those skill sets. That would lead to thought redundancy, which slows the creative thinking process necessary for productive gain. Some may have similar strengths and share some weaknesses, but the way they have experienced life and learning is as unique as fingerprints.

"Therefore, when a team of workers gather, each member brings their personalized gifts to share. The other team members, having observed this sharing, learn and grow in the area of the sharing member's uniqueness and expertise. The culture that's created by a company plays heavily into the success of the results it consistently produces. When the culture of a company promotes people walking into a meeting with an openness to what they will learn and gain from their teammates during the meeting, along with being prepared to teach others with their own contribution to the meeting, *great things happen.*

"This same concept can occur with any family at the kitchen table, where families have a meeting opportunity at least once, maybe more, each day. A meeting at the kitchen table might begin with the open question, 'How are you better today than you were yesterday?' with each person answering regarding an area of life they grew and learned more about that day. Then the other family members get to share in that growth without having to experience exactly what the person sharing did. All of what I've just explained is just a small part of what Group Mentoring can mean.

"Here are some additional examples where the benefits of mentoring can occur in a group setting. On nonprofit and for-profit boards of directors. Typically, boards are made up of people with diverse backgrounds, meaning, if you have the privilege of serving on one, you'll have an opportunity to learn from an expert in an area that isn't one of your strengths. You'll also be able to share with others in your own personal area of expertise.

"Small businesses normally aren't able to form a typical board of directors. However, they can from what I call a 'pseudo-board,' made up of their banker, CPA, attorney, and insurance agent, bringing all of them together to share their expertise with each other for the benefit of the company. Group mentoring also occurs when you're a part of a breakout group that's been given a set task. One of the first things this group should do is determine the available skill sets of each person and let them contribute to the challenge in the way they can be the most help. Group mentoring can also take root if you belong to civic clubs like Rotary, Lions, or Kiwanis. The local chamber of commerce provides oodles of opportunities for group mentoring."

Martha gave Antonio a thank-you wink when he said that last one. He continued, "The key is developing a routine or system to prepare yourself and others before any group gathering, so you become aware of mentoring opportunities the moment they arise. You train yourself to know what you're looking for. It's like when you purchase a silver SUV and suddenly notice all of the other people that drive silver SUVs. You notice *now* because you have a reason to notice. My group mentoring gains in life have been an important part of my overall mentoring experience.

"I've covered the four types of mentoring with you so far today, but there's one more related subject I'd like to cover with you. It may allow both of us an opportunity to put mentoring into action in a way that could change the world. I feel like it's the true purpose of us meeting here today."

Martha paused, looking at the kind, caring, and hope-filled face of the person across the table. She began to silently wonder where today would fit on her Greatest Day of Her Life chart. She settled on Top Seven for sure and finally said to him, "Antonio, you couldn't budge me from this table if you tried … except for one thing. I'm a Type-1 diabetic, and I can sense my blood sugar going a little low. I can stay here until closing if it means I can keep learning from *you*. But I do need to grab one of the delicious baked goods from Gigi. May I bring one back for you?"

Antonio smiled and said, "Yes. Please. It will be good to take a break for a few minutes and practice some mentoring conversation. Gigi knows what my favorite is, and don't worry about paying. Gigi will add it to my bill."

After eating their sweet treats, getting refills for their drinks, and learning much more about each other, Martha could sense that Antonio had something on his heart that he wanted to share. She provided the opening for him by saying, "I know you have more to share. Please continue." Antonio smiled as he felt the appreciation, respect, and caring heart that Martha was sharing with him through unspoken words that she was communicating in other ways.

"One of my favorite mentors, who for decades helped guide my career and personal life, worked for one of the largest banking organizations in the state, which is headquartered right here in our community. His career had led him to the top of the executive list, and his daily contribution to the success of the bank was unmatched … *until* the day he turned sixty-five and was forced by company policy to retire. Here he was at the very top of his game, with the highest ROI of any of the 1,600-plus employees the bank employed, and his career came to a forced ending. He was financially set for life and didn't need to work, but I couldn't help but wonder why our society has this notion that someone retires … and that's that. I get the whole, 'We need new blood, fresh ideas, and youth to keep this company moving forward,' but shouldn't someone's value to a company be based on what they can contribute, regardless of age? This led me to think even deeper about this. A little research told me that *our community,* being the world headquarters of a company with a high percentage of research scientists, *has the highest number of PhDs per capita in the entire United States.* We also have the highest number of engineers per capita. We're loaded with highly educated people that are aptly trained at being successful problem-solvers. Some, after a successful career, retire as early as fifty-five years old and choose to stay in our community. I realized we have this massive, incredible, and capable asset that, for the most part, isn't being utilized at all."

Antonio was on a roll, and Martha's mind was running like a thoroughbred trying to keep up. It was an interesting story, but where was he going with this?

"Your organization puts about forty-five people through a leadership program each year, doesn't it?"

"That's correct."

"And share with me its purpose."

"Sure. We attempt to identify people who will be future leaders in their industry and have potential to share those leadership skills with our community. Over three days we expose them to our public school system, the inner workings of our city and county government, our court system, nearly every nonprofit that serves our community, and our law enforcement agencies. We also attempt to show them all of the amenities our community offers to its residents, including the Center for Performing Arts, the library, the nature center, the recycling center, the toboggan run and hiking/biking trails, the community center, and the extensive park system. At the end of the program, we invite each participant to find an organization or cause that may have found a place in their heart and get involved in the positive impact that organization has on the greater community."

Antonio asked a follow-up question: "And isn't there a leadership program designed for high school students?"

"There is. It's one that we created and then spun off so that it could be run by the students with help from—and I know you'll like this—adult mentors. The program utilizes team-building exercises, responsibility and accountability training, and personal development—all designed to supplement their education and provide leadership training in hopes that they'll take a strong leadership role in whatever they pursue in life."

Antonio asked, "Are you pleased with the results of these programs?"

"Yes. Absolutely yes. We've tracked the data going back the thirty years the adult program has been in place, and we've been able to quantify the impact the program has had on our community."

Antonio projected a warm smile and then began his pitch. "Martha, what if I told you that I believed I could offer the opportunity of a similar program, based on a different demographic, that could change the world?"

The friendship between the two had found its footing and there was now a flow to their banter. "Speak on, Antonio, speak on. You have my indivisible, which is young-person talk for undivided, attention."

Antonio chuckled. The young-person talk had made for a pleasant moment. He was now ready to toss his idea over the net at Martha and see where it landed.

"Martha, I believe that every community has an asset that is completely untapped. It's comprised of what you young whippersnappers like to call 'old people.' Once people reach the age of about thirty, they tend to dislike the aging process. I've grown to embrace and love the aging process by focusing on the positives and ignoring the negatives of aging. The amount of wisdom a person accumulates in the first sixty years of their life is astronomical. The only challenge is finding others willing to listen and be mentored … which is strange, because it's that wisdom, from someone who has already lived a mistake, that can prevent a multitude of mistakes that someone younger is about to live. Given that roughly one-quarter of our population is sixty or older, I would like to create a program, modeled after your Community Leadership Program, that focuses on seniors. We could call it 'Senior Leadership,' and it would heavily recruit those who have retired or are about to retire and offer an opportunity to utilize the four types of mentoring, taking advantage of the wisdom they've acquired over their lives so far. The ultimate goal would be to develop a program that has such a powerful positive impact on our community that it could be replicated by every community in the country and, eventually, the world."

Martha asked, "So it's kind of a 'start small, think really big' kind of program? I'm both intrigued and interested. I have to admit you are very persuasive, and I'll be doggone if you haven't convinced me to the point that I believe everything you've shared with me today. Your thought process is solid. Execution will be the key. Tell you what, Antonio: If you are willing to commit to holding monthly seminars based on the four types of mentoring through the Chamber, open to all members of the community, then I would be willing to work directly with you to create the curriculum and agenda for our new Senior Leadership Program that we can replicate and offer to communities all over the world. Is it a deal?"

Antonio took in the moment. He had been told not to mention to Martha until later that he had stopped at the Answer Discovery a half hour before her and that the offer she had just presented to him was the gift he had asked for. Antonio stuck his hand out to shake Martha's and said, "It will be our greatest adventure. It's a deal!"

Martha firmly shook Antonio's hand and replied, "Thank you for sharing **The Gift of Mentoring** with me today. We're going to do great things together."

THE GIFT OF GRATITUDE

B rian got out of his ten-year-old Lexus SUV. It had 136,000 miles on it and had served him well since he'd purchased it three years ago. He couldn't help but smile, thinking about how some people would see his vehicle and automatically make assumptions about him because of the make. He knew he was just as guilty as he pondered other people's lives based on what they drove. He fell victim to the assumption game, just like everyone else, subconsciously analyzing every available nugget of information as quickly as he could to form an opinion that made him either want to avoid, investigate further, or remain neutral and just move on. Did they have tattoos? What was their choice of footwear? Clothing? Hairstyle? Nail maintenance? Did they care about what others thought of them? Were they in great shape or not-so-great shape? What was their childhood like? Were they LGBTQ+ or hetero? Were they in a hurry? Impatient? Compassionate? Kind? Caring? Religious? Faithful? A parent? Gainfully employed? Did they like their job? Had sports had an impact on their life? What were they committed to?

Brian knew he was committed to this quick analysis whenever he was around other people. It was almost like a game he played with himself. He was an engineer, after all, and he was in love with the strategy of logic and the role it played in decision-making. It's why he drove a vehicle that he deduced had the best return on investment (or ROI, as he liked to call it) based on safety, value, comfort, and resale value. He had also learned that what some people called intuition or a gut feeling about something was, in reality, nothing more than subconscious pattern recognition that we all rely on every day of our life when making decisions and coming to conclusions. It was what had led him to the Answer Discovery that day. As he was about to enter the building, he reminded himself to be extremely observant of everything that was about to happen while staying focused on what he wanted to achieve while being there.

As Brian entered and took his first three steps inside, his planned strategy kind of blew up when his engineer-trained mind picked up that he had just been welcomed by name but could not figure out how that had just happened. None of his preconceived notions about what he would experience were happening, and his subconscious pattern recognition seemed to be on vacation at the particular moment. He loved logic and had to skip a beat to get back to being present in the moment. He knew precisely why he was here. He worked for a large corporation. He loved his job and was good at it. He was more than fairly compensated. He wanted to believe that he was making a difference, but the company was so large it was hard to compute any real impact he may have been making on the world around him. He had begun to think more about his purpose in life, wanting to make more of a difference in his community outside of work, but he had absolutely no clue as to how he might make that happen given the particular skill sets he possessed.

So GLAD YOU'RE HERE TODAY, BRIAN. YOU'RE GOING TO HAVE A POWERFUL IMPACT ON THE WORLD AS YOU CONTINUE FORWARD IN LIFE.

Brian had to fight the urge to figure out how this communication was happening. It was so strange. Yet he had just heard some encouraging words. It's almost as if his reason for being there was known before he had even entered. "I'd like to make a difference in the world but I'm not sure how to go about that," he responded very simply.

IN TWO HOURS YOU'LL ARRIVE AT 3012 ELMHURST ROAD AND FIND YOURSELF IN THE PARKING LOT OF A COMPANY NAMED LIFE-STYLE GARMENT CARE. YOU'LL ENTER THE BUSINESS AND ASK FOR THE OWNER, WHOSE NAME IS DUTCH LAMAR. HE'LL BE EXPECTING YOU, AND HE WILL SET YOU FORTH ON A PATH POINTED IN THE DIRECTION YOU WANT TO HEAD.

OVER THE NEXT TWO HOURS, BEFORE YOU ARRIVE AT THE CLEANERS, YOU'LL SPEND THAT TIME LEARNING HOW PEOPLE WHO MEDITATE ARE ABLE TO CLEAR THEIR MINDS OF ALL THOUGHTS IN ORDER TO ALLOW THE THOUGHTS ABOUT TO BE PRESENTED TO THEM FILL THE OPEN SPACE. IT'S REALLY A SYSTEM OF REMOVING OBSTACLES THAT MAY LEAD TO QUICK CONCLUSIONS, WHICH MAY BE FALSE CONCLUSIONS WHEN WE'RE ATTEMPTING TO LEARN SOMETHING NEW.

YOUR ENGINEERING BACKGROUND CAN JUST AS EASILY WORK *FOR* YOU AS WORK AGAINST YOU IF YOU WILL ALLOW YOUR MIND TO ABSORB FIRST, ORGANIZE SECOND, DEVELOP STRATEGY THIRD, AND PUT THE STRATEGY INTO PRACTICE PRIOR TO ANY ATTEMPT TO MEASURE OUTCOMES BEFORE THE RESULTS EVEN OCCUR. ENJOY THE EXPERIENCE, BRIAN.

As Brian left the Answer Discovery and headed towards his vehicle, his mind was on fire. He had really appreciated how direct and precise his instructions had been as his day was about to continue. One thing that concerned him is that he was being sent to a dry cleaner. Having never stepped foot in a dry cleaner before, he wasn't even sure what a dry cleaner exactly did. The other piece that seemed missing from the puzzle was how in the world a dry cleaner named Dutch might be able to provide the answer to how he could make a bigger difference.

Halfway between the Answer Discovery and Lifestyle Garment Care, Brian pulled into the local library, where he could spend the next couple of hours preparing for his meeting by researching the whole meditation angle. He had had some brief liaisons with meditation but was never interested to committing to the proclaimed benefits of what daily meditation promised. It went back to the ROI that he based all of his daily actions on. He just couldn't justify the time meditation required for the benefits it supposedly provided. However, after hearing about the apparent significance of clearing his mind before the meeting in the Answer Discovery, he had reason to question his previous conclusion about the practice.

Brian enjoyed his two hours in the library immensely, having gained a lot of what he called "new knowledge." It was one more success that he could credit to this day. Then he was back on the road, and after a five-minute ride he pulled into a lot in front of a building with a big sign out front bearing what appeared to be a rising sun. Underneath that was the name of the company, LIFESTYLE GARMENT CARE, and underneath the name was a tagline that read RISING BEYOND EXPECTATIONS. This was going to be interesting.

· · ·

As Brian entered the store, he glanced around at the environment. He could swear he smelled fresh-baked cookies and, sure enough, he spied a small tabletop convection oven with a full cooling rack sitting right next to it, holding a dozen cookies. Just to the right of that he noticed a five-shelf display of books with a sign above that read LENDING LIBRARY – PLEASE HELP YOURSELF TO A BETTER LIFE. Then a bright and cheerful young lady whose nametag said CHARLOTTE came forward from a sliding door into the space and said, "Wonderful morning. Any chance your name is Brian?"

Brian, a little astonished, replied, "Yes, yes it is … but how did you know?"

Charlotte responded with a big smile, "We've been expecting you. Welcome to our slice of the world. It's a fine slice, even if I do say so myself. Having someone visit us is one of our favorite things here at Lifestyle Garment Care. Let me grab our coach and connect the two of you."

Charlotte was only gone about twenty seconds when a man came bounding through the sliding door that separated the workspace from the front area. "Brian, I'm so grateful you're here today. I'm Dutch. Welcome, welcome … wow, so good to have you here. Here, please have a fresh-baked 'stress reducer.' I call them that because the word *cookie* doesn't properly convey what they do. They're guaranteed to improve your day. Come on back to our production area so I can introduce you to our team. They're the finest group of individuals working in our industry."

As Dutch spent two to three minutes introducing all ten members of the team to him, Brian noticed three things that consistently occurred during those introductions. First, Dutch always said how much he appreciated the role that person played on the team. Second, he mentioned how much respect he had for their unique contribution toward the overall goals of the company. And third, he emphasized what a privilege it was to be able to be their coach. Brian had a sense that there existed a very unique culture here at this place—an incredible culture he never would have imagined could have existed at a business like a dry cleaner.

After introducing all of his team, Dutch led Brian to his office. As Brian walked in, he found an office whose four walls were covered with bookcases over six feet in height. "There must be over five hundred books on all of these shelves. Have you read them all?" Brian asked.

"Sure have. Some more than once. They've been an important part of my character development over my journey as an adult. *So* important, in fact, that I've purchased and given away somewhere between three and four thousand books over the years. Every time I'm with a person, if our discussion coincides with a lesson I've learned from a particular book, I give them a copy of that book. I keep a mini-library in the back of my vehicle of about thirty of my favorites just for that reason."

The engineer part of Brian's mind was first attempting to do the math behind the cost of three to four thousand books, but he made the leap to wondering what the impact may have been from thousands of people receiving a book that was tailored just to them and what they were thinking about at that particular moment when Dutch had given them the book.

Brian was attempting to analyze if he had ever previously been in the presence of someone as unique as this Dutch Lamar, but his thoughts were interrupted when all of a sudden Dutch asked him, "Have you ever thought about the studies that prove that more people die from loneliness each year than smoking? I was at a seminar related to people with disabilities when I first heard that. I don't recall much of what the speaker that day said after that. That statement consumed my mind. I started thinking about people I knew who had passed away and began to clearly understand that loneliness had played a major role with several of them in their decline to death. I began to wonder how many death certificates in the world should have had 'loneliness' as the cause of death. Then, having learned through personal experience that lasting and solid friendship for people with disabilities was the number one concern they had, I realized that this issue wasn't just a concern for people with disabilities but for *all* people. As humans, we're not very well-equipped to handle loneliness. We need others to be active participants in each of our lives on a consistent basis."

As Dutch paused for a second, Brian took a brief moment to be grateful that he had spent the previous two hours pursuing the benefits of meditation and clearing his mind. This man in front of him was different than anyone else he had ever experienced before. Brian was able to adapt to this unique environment he now found himself in and wanted to engage at an even deeper level.

Brian was staring intently at Dutch. He had been hanging on his every word, and he noticed a tear running down each side of Dutch's face. "Wow!" was all Brian could muster. Dutch wanted to transition and move past the sadness of people dying from loneliness and asked Brian if he wanted to enjoy a cold bottle of water. Brian accepted, and both of them took a few pulls before getting back to the purpose of Brian's visit.

Brian attempted to move the conversation forward with, "So this whole 'loneliness causes more deaths each year than smoking' thought process... where did all of that lead you?" Dutch was pleased with the question. He knew that teaching someone required a certain flow, and right now the two of them were humming along nicely.

"I knew I wanted to make a difference—a significant difference—and now I was armed with the belief that, even if I only had a powerful positive impact on one person's life, *it counted!* I also had a little advantage, being a dry cleaner."

"How so?" Brian questioned.

"Well, I hate to say it, but: low expectations. You see, my experience is that people in our industry are looked down upon as compared to glamorous jobs like being an engineer." Dutch winked at Brian when he said the word *engineer.* "Rather than taking offense to this, I always saw it as a positive, believing that there wasn't even a remote chance that I *couldn't* surpass those low expectations. I compared it to being asked to high jump over a snake."

Dutch let out a hearty laugh. Brian was glad he did because he was trying to suppress his own laughter. His admiration for this man skyrocketed as he realized that Dutch wasn't worried about what people who didn't know him thought of him, but focused on being a change agent for the betterment of himself and others.

Dutch took a long swallow of water and continued, "I knew that we had a large customer base that could provide me a captive audience. I decided that I had an opportunity to put something in each customer's hand every time they picked up an order. I knew that I was risking our reputation and that whatever I did would be used to define the character of our company. It had to be positive, useful, and significant. I also knew I had to be creative and come up with something no one else had ever done before. I examined my life and the things that meant the most to me, and I settled on what may be my best idea ever ... *so far!*" Dutch was smiling and Brian could tell that Dutch was super passionate about everything he was describing. "I decided I would call it a Life Enhancement Kit, and I got busy right away in its development."

Brian interrupted, "A Life Enhancement Kit?"

"You heard me right." Dutch was on an roll. "The kit would be contained in a bright yellow nine-by-twelve envelope with our logo and the words Life Enhancement Kit in big, bold, navy blue letters screaming at you on the front. Inside it would include three components. The first component was a letter explaining what the kit's intentions were for the person in possession of it, how the kit would work to enhance their life, including the benefits to them and others when utilized, and, most importantly, why they should consider taking immediate action putting the kit to work. The second was a bright yellow greeting card of sorts that on the front had the word Thank on top of the word You, with an exclamation point below. It was designed to quickly capture a person's attention and nearly force them to open the card to see what it said inside. On the right half of the inside, the card had a statement across the top that said THANK YOU FOR HELPING ME! Directly underneath were 'to' and 'from' fields to be filled out by the person initiating the action, and below that was a sentence that read, I AM GIVING YOU THIS CARD BECAUSE I AM SO VERY GRATEFUL THAT YOU HAVE HAD A POSITIVE IMPACT ON MY LIFE. HERE'S HOW. Fifteen lines of blank spaces provided a chance to tell the person *how* they had had an impact and the results that their impact produced. At the very bottom of those lines was a final sentence that read, HELPING OTHER PEOPLE IS A GIFT THAT EVERYONE CAN SHARE. THANKS AGAIN FOR SHARING YOUR GIFT WITH ME! The third component to the kit was a bright yellow envelope that the card could be placed in, designed to stand out from all the other mail someone might receive. This all sounds pretty crazy, right?"

Brian, whose mind was keeping up as best it could, replied, "Yeah, a little bit."

Dutch continued on like a man having just completed a second pot of coffee might. "That's precisely the point. If you study human behavior, you begin to notice certain things that trigger everyone's curiosity gene. Every person we handed one of these Life Enhancement Kit envelopes to couldn't resist looking inside. I mean, think about it. Is there anyone who *isn't* interested in enhancing their life if there's an easy way to do it?"

"I suppose not. But weren't you concerned that people wouldn't follow through all the way with sending someone the card?"

"That's a legitimate question, Brian. First of all, knowing that they couldn't resist reading the letter inside, I already had my first success in establishing, with that particular individual, the character of our company and all of our team members. Secondly, I instituted the 'starfish story' line of thinking, believing that if only one person followed all the way through with sending the card, then both their life and life of the recipient had been enhanced. That made it a complete success, and one way that I was able to make a difference in the world. There's some additional information I can share about this Life Enhancement Kit that brought us great joy. We were all amazed at how many of our customers came back to us and asked for additional kits. One person asked us for twenty-five, which we were thrilled to give them. Other people told us that they loved the idea, but instead of sending the card they ended up sending emails and text messages to people that had made a difference and were able to experience the joy that the spirit of the kits intended."

Brian took the opportunity of Dutch pausing for a second to fill in some blanks in his inquisitive mind. "I'm super-curious with the results you seem to have achieved. What was it that the letter said that moved people to taking immediate action?"

Dutch was very pleased with this question from Brian. He was beginning to sense that this relationship that began today would morph into a friendship that would bring both of them great joy.

"That's another wonderful question, Brian. I've learned that if someone is expected to read an entire page of dialogue, the first sentence better hit a home run, or they'll never come close to reading it all. It's the same with giving a speech. The goal is to capture your target audience's attention right at the beginning and never let go. I spent a lot of time creating that first sentence, and in the end it was one that told exactly what I felt in my heart. At the top of the letter, it read, EVERYTHING I AM AND ALL OF MY SUCCESS, I OWE TO OTHERS. That statement set the tone of what followed.

"The first paragraph talked about two beliefs I have. The first belief is the complete truth, which my life has proved, behind the famous Zig Ziglar quote: 'You can get everything you want in life if you help enough *other* people get what they want.' The second belief I have is that '*Gratitude* is one of the most powerful tools every person possesses in the pursuit of living a wonderful, significant, and fulfilling life.'

"The second paragraph explained that I had gone on a mission to thank every person that I felt had had a significant and positive impact on my life. I included all of the unique ways I went about accomplishing this and emphasized that, as a result, this small and simple gesture of thanking people had had a *huge positive impact* on their lives (and in turn, on mine). I was able to live the joy twice.

"Near the bottom I included a quote from John F. Kennedy: ONE PERSON CAN MAKE A DIFFERENCE AND EVERY PERSON SHOULD TRY, which reminded me, again, of the starfish story. Then I finished with some heartfelt encouragement to take immediate action in four simple steps:

1. Think about someone who's made a difference.
2. Fill out the card.
3. Place in the envelope included.
4. Mail it.

"When you really think about this attempt to make a difference, you can't come up with a downside."

It was Brian's turn to reflect. "Being an engineer, it isn't often that I would use these words, but I am officially blown away. This seems like the kind of idea that, if it caught on, could change the world for the better."

"Well, what it really did was enhance the culture of our team and our customers. Many of our customers would take the Life Enhancement Kit home and have long family discussions about every possible outcome embracing gratitude, and thanking others, could have. There have been so many additional benefits like that that I didn't anticipate when the idea first germinated in my mind."

"So this was a huge idea for you," Brian offered. "Have there been any others?"

"Lots!" Dutch exclaimed. "But I'll focus on one that came from this one. When we first started distributing the Life Enhancement Kits, we began to receive a lot of positive feedback. This stoked the fire inside all of our team, and they decided they wanted to pursue unique ways to make a difference in the world. One team member came up with the idea that we could attach to every order a Thought for the Day that consisted of things to be grateful for in our community. That continues to have a positive impact on the community we serve and has grown to be part of a subscription email or text that people sign up for. I share that specific example because it was an idea that was motivated by and that grew out of the Life Enhancement Kit idea. There have been many others, and because of this process, every person that is a member of our team takes great pride in who they are, what they represent, and the character of the company they work for. It's a wonderful, significant, and fulfilling way to live life every day."

Brian had a look on his face that made Dutch think there was still something that lingered in that engineer-trained mind. Brian spoke up. "So Dutch, how do you think the Life Enhancement Kit relates to how you started this conversation, telling me that studies show that more people die from loneliness than from smoking?" Brian was, in essence, asking Dutch to tie their meeting together from beginning to end. It was all that Dutch had hoped for, and he realized that Brian had already trained his brain to clearly see the preferred results of the big picture while understanding all of the smaller steps necessary to get there.

"That's a pertinent question, Brian. Thanks for asking. Here's how the Life Enhancement Kit became part of the 'eliminating loneliness in the world' puzzle. I had mentioned how customers began sharing positive stories as a result of utilizing the Life Enhancement Kit, which is what inspired our team here to seek other ways to positively impact our community.

"One of the offshoots was the Thought for the Day notes we gave to each customer when they picked their orders up. One of the Thought for the Day notes that we passed out to customers read, CURE LONELINESS IN THE WORLD BY SENDING TWO SENTENCES OF ENCOURAGEMENT AND LOVE TO TWO PEOPLE. THE TWO PEOPLE SHOULD INCLUDE ONE PERSON YOU KNOW AND ONE PERSON YOU HAVE YET TO KNOW.

"This particular Thought for the Day took off and began to run. Customers came back to us and shared what happened after they sent just two sentences of encouragement and love, and the stories were incredible. Many of those notes made it into the hands of people in nursing homes and assisted living facilities. They traced the concept back to us and enlisted our help in having all of their residents and staff send two sentences to two people each and every day. Owners of similar facilities in other communities witnessed a huge change in the people and staff in our community and began to promote the program at *all* of their facilities.

"Pretty soon the simple concept began to travel around the country as word got out about the positive change that occurred in the people who participated on a regular basis. Some teachers witnessed the power this simple program was having and began utilizing the concept with their students. There were so many 'teachable outcomes' that teachers committed to making it part of the curriculum in their school districts. The local nonprofit in our community that advocated for people with disabilities told us that much of their membership was receiving two-sentence notes from others in the community. Their staff created a program to help all of the people *they* served to embrace sending two sentences to two people each and every day.

"What was most incredible is that it appeared that this simple strategy, when used daily, became the part of the day people most looked forward to and found the most reward from of all of the things they did each day. The concept has become a valuable 'tool for life' that's free and available to everyone, and, most importantly, it's brought about positive change in the world and greatly reduced loneliness. Funny how that Thought for the Day turned into Thought for a Happy Life.

"It then occurred to me that we should capture these stories. That set me about the task of capturing, organizing, and writing about the stories with the result being the series of books I have written, entitled *The Answer Discovery: How to Change the World by Helping Others... and Ourselves.*

"I'd like to give you the first book in the series. I've already written a two-sentence note in the front of it to encourage you to pursue your desire to make a difference in the world. I know that you will. So today I offer you **The Gift of Gratitude**. You wouldn't be here today if there wasn't a great belief in you. I want you to know that I believe in you. And I want to be available to you any time you need me."

Brian was so moved by the emotions he was feeling that he suddenly realized that tears were rolling down both of his cheeks. He gathered himself together as he realized his time there with this incredible man was coming to an end. Brian looked deeply at Dutch's face and said, "One last thing before I leave. Is there any chance you have an extra Life Enhancement Kit you could give me? I have a special person I'd like to send a thank-you note to."

ACKNOWLEDGMENTS

The following people believed in me and supported me right from the time I began writing. Their inspiration and encouragement propelled me forward each day. Each of them played a unique role in helping me bring these gifts to each person who reads this book. I'm grateful for their unwavering support. In no particular order, they are: Dom Monastiere, David Rosenstock, Bob Ribble, Michael "Stucky" Szczotka, Kate Hessling, Dave Clark, Dan Chalk, Candi Miller, Uncle Fred Rusher, Tom Luplow, John Haag, Chris Tointon, Wally Mayton, Dave Dittenber, George Anderson, Pete Shaheen, Jeff Rekeweg, Courtney Jerome, and the New England Sanitone Group. There are many others, and if you're reading this thinking that I could have included your name, please know that your name, and the contribution you've made in my life, is recorded in my heart.

From day one, the contribution my wife *Kim* has made to this book is immeasurable. She has read every word several times, provided positive feedback, and kept me focused on the big picture of the positive impact this book is intended to have on the world. Also, in full support have been our four sons, our daughter-in-law, my four siblings and their families, and many cousins.

Finally, I'd like to acknowledge YOU! Reading this book has helped the "movement" I've created allowing people to discover consistent joy and happiness through helping others ... and thus, themselves.

Always know that I Believe in YOU!
It's time to GiddyUp!

ABOUT THE AUTHOR

Paul White credits "an insatiable curiosity" for the successes he's been able to achieve in his life. Those successes include entrepreneurialism, owning a thriving business, professional sales and marketing, public speaking, being a syndicated columnist, and more. At the root of all his efforts is the Zig Ziglar quote, "You can get everything you want in life, if you just help enough other people get what they want," which Paul has embraced in every area of his life.

You can learn more about Paul at his website
www.theanswerdiscovery.com